NIAGARA FALLS TRAVEL GUIDE

2024

55+ Fun and Cool Things to Do in and Around Niagara Falls

Taylor Allen

All rights reserved. No part of this book may be reproduced, stored in a retrieval system, or transmitted in any form or by any means, electronic, mechanical, photocopying, recording, or otherwise, without the prior written permission of the copyright owner. The information contained in this book is for general information purposes only. The author and publisher make no representations or warranties of any kind, express or implied, about the completeness, accuracy, reliability, suitability or availability with respect to the book or the information, products, services, or related graphics contained in the book for any purpose. Any reliance you place on such information is therefore strictly at your own risk.

Copyright © 2023 by Taylor Allen.

TABLE OF CONTENT

Chapter 1: Introduction _____ 7
    Why Niagara Falls? _____ 8
    A Brief History _____ 9

Chapter 2: Getting Ready for Adventure _____ 13
    Packing Essentials _____ 13
    Best Times to Visit _____ 15
    Navigating the Area _____ 17

Chapter 3: The Majestic Niagara Falls _____ 21
    Up-Close with the Falls _____ 21
    Behind the Scenes: Tours and Facts _____ 23
    Capturing the Perfect Photo _____ 24

Chapter 4: On the Water _____ 27
    Maid of the Mist: A Classic Experience _____ 27
    Jet Boating Thrills _____ 29
    Exploring the Islands _____ 31

Chapter 5: Land Adventures _____ 35
    Hiking Trails with a View _____ 35
    Biking Around the Falls _____ 36
    Zip-lining Over the Gorge _____ 38

Chapter 6: Entertainment Beyond the Falls _____ 41
    Clifton Hill: The Entertainment Hub _____ 41
    Casino Nights _____ 43
    Festivals and Events _____ 45

Chapter 7: Culinary Delights _____ 49
Dining with a View _____ 49
Local Flavors to Try _____ 51
Sweet Treats _____ 53

Chapter 8: Family-Friendly Fun _____ 57
Adventure Parks _____ 57
Butterfly Conservatory _____ 58
Educational Excursions _____ 60

Chapter 9: Nightlife by the Falls _____ 63
Waterfront Bars _____ 63
Nighttime Illumination _____ 64
Stargazing Over the Falls _____ 66

Chapter 10: Hidden Gems _____ 69
Off the Beaten Path _____ 69
Secret Scenic Spots _____ 70
Local Favorites _____ 73

Chapter 11: Day Trips and Beyond _____ 77
Exploring Nearby Towns _____ 77
Winery Tours _____ 79
Adventure Across the Border _____ 80

Chapter 12: Relaxation and Wellness _____ 85
Spas with a View _____ 85
Yoga Retreats _____ 86

Chapter 13: Adrenaline Adventures _____ 89

    Helicopter Rides _____ 89
    White-Water Rafting _____ 90
    Ziplining Across the Gorge _____ 92

Chapter 14: Winter Wonders _____ *95*
    Frozen Falls: A Winter Wonderland _____ 95
    Ice Skating Near the Falls _____ 97
    Cozy Winter Retreats _____ 99

Chapter 15: Cultural Immersion _____ *101*
    Indigenous Heritage Experiences _____ 101
    Art Galleries and Exhibitions _____ 103
    Local Workshops and Classes _____ 105

Chapter 16: Eco-Friendly Explorations ____ *109*
    Nature Reserves and Parks _____ 109
    Bird Watching by the Falls _____ 111

Chapter 17: Romance by the Falls _____ *115*
    Romantic Dining Spots _____ 115
    Sunset Cruises _____ 116
    Enchanting Proposal Locations _____ 118

Chapter 18: Haunted Niagara _____ *121*
    Ghost Tours and Legends _____ 121
    Spooky Sites to Explore _____ 122
    Paranormal Experiences _____ 124

Chapter 19: Waterfront Relaxation _____ *127*
    Lakeside Retreats _____ 127

Fishing Adventures _____ 128
Picnic Spots with a View _____ 130
Chapter 20: Travel Itinerary _____ *133*
Family Friendly Itinerary _____ 133
Art and Culture Itinerary _____ 137
Romantic Itinerary _____ 141
Food and Wine Itinerary _____ 144
Historical Itinerary _____ 148
Outdoor Adventure Itinerary _____ 152
Chapter 21: Planning Your Next Visit _____ *159*
Tips for Return Travelers _____ 159
Seasonal Highlights _____ 161
Making Lasting Memories _____ 164

Disclaimer: Kindly Read This Notice Before You Continue

Step into the pages of this travel guide and prepare for a truly extraordinary experience. Delve into the captivating world of Niagara Falls where imagination, creativity, and a thirst for adventure reign supreme. You won't find any images within these pages, as we firmly believe in the power of firsthand exploration, devoid of visual filters or preconceptions. Each monument, every nook and cranny eagerly awaits your arrival, ready to astonish and amaze. Why spoil the thrill of that initial glimpse, that overwhelming sense of wonder? So get ready to embark on an unparalleled journey, where your imagination becomes the sole means of transportation and you, the ultimate guide. Release any preconceived notions and allow yourself to be transported to an authentic Niagara Falls experience brimming with hidden treasures. Let the enchantment commence, but remember, the most breathtaking images will be the ones painted by your own eyes.

Unlike many conventional guides, this book needs no detailed maps. Why, you may ask? Because we firmly believe that the truest discoveries happen when you wander, when you surrender to the current of the surroundings and embrace the uncertainty of the path. No rigid itineraries or precise directions are provided here, for we yearn for you to explore Niagara Falls on your own terms, unbound by limitations or restrictions. Surrender yourself to the currents and unearth hidden gems that no map could reveal. Be audacious, follow your instincts, and brace yourself for serendipitous encounters. The magic of the journey commences now, within a world without maps, where roads materialize with each step and the most extraordinary adventures await in the folds of the unknown.

Chapter 1: Introduction

Welcome to the mesmerizing world of "55+ Fun Things to Do in and Around the Niagara Falls"! In the heart of nature's grandeur, where the rhythmic roar of cascading waters meets the thrill of endless adventures, this guide invites you to embark on an unforgettable journey through the wonders of Niagara.

As you turn the pages, you'll discover not just a compendium of activities but a curated collection of experiences that promise to redefine your notion of fun. Why Niagara Falls, you may ask? Beyond the iconic beauty of the falls lies a region teeming with excitement, culture, and hidden gems waiting to be explored.

Our journey begins with an exploration of the falls themselves—delving into the mystique of their history, the sheer power they exude, and the myriad ways you can immerse yourself in their majesty. From heart-pounding boat rides to serene island explorations, Chapter 3 sets the stage for the adventure that awaits.

But this guide isn't just about the falls; it's a comprehensive manual for every type of traveler. Whether you seek the adrenaline rush of water adventures, the tranquility of scenic hikes, or the pulsating energy of the nightlife, each chapter unfolds a new facet of Niagara's charm.

Picture yourself soaring above the gorge on a zip line or savoring exquisite culinary delights with a panoramic view of the falls. Imagine the laughter of your family echoing in adventure parks or the quiet moments of relaxation in a spa with the falls as your backdrop. This guide is your key to unlocking these moments and more.

From family-friendly escapades to romantic rendezvous, cultural immersions to eco-friendly explorations, our chapters weave a tapestry of possibilities. As you read on, you'll find practical tips, local insights, and the kind of information that transforms a trip into an experience.

So, whether you're a first-time visitor or a seasoned traveler returning to this natural wonder, "55 Fun Things to Do in and Around the Niagara Falls" is your passport to a world where every moment is an adventure waiting to happen. Get ready to be captivated, inspired, and, most importantly, to have the time of your life in the enchanting embrace of Niagara.

Why Niagara Falls?

Niagara Falls, a natural wonder nestled on the border of the United States and Canada, captivates the hearts of millions with its sheer grandeur and breathtaking beauty. The allure of Niagara is not merely in the cascading waters but in the profound experience it offers to every visitor.

Nature's Spectacle: At the heart of the allure is, of course, the magnificent falls themselves. The raw power and beauty of the cascading water create a spectacle that transcends the ordinary. Witnessing the falls in person, feeling the mist on your face, and hearing the roaring sound is an encounter with nature's grandeur that words often fail to capture.

Iconic Landmarks: Beyond the falls, Niagara is adorned with iconic landmarks like the Horseshoe Falls, American Falls, and Bridal Veil Falls. Each has its own unique character, contributing to the overall tapestry of this natural masterpiece.

Cross-Border Charm: Straddling the border between the United States and Canada, Niagara Falls is a symbol of international harmony. The falls can be admired from both the American and Canadian sides, each offering a distinct perspective. The Rainbow Bridge, connecting the two countries, adds a touch of cross-cultural charm to the experience.

Historical Significance: Niagara Falls carries a rich historical legacy. From the indigenous communities that revered it to the daring adventurers who navigated its waters, the falls have witnessed centuries of human history. Exploring this history adds depth to the visit, connecting you to a tapestry of stories that have unfolded against the backdrop of the falls.

A Multisensory Experience: Visiting Niagara is not just a visual feast; it's a multisensory experience. The sound of rushing water, the feel of mist on your skin, and the vibrant colors of the falls illuminated at night create a sensory symphony that lingers in memory long after the visit.

A Brief History

Niagara Falls, one of the world's most iconic natural wonders, has a rich and fascinating history that spans centuries. The story of Niagara Falls is not just about the majestic cascades but also the cultural, geological, and human elements that have shaped its narrative.

The geological history of Niagara Falls dates back over 12,000 years to the end of the last Ice Age. As the massive glaciers retreated, they carved out the Great Lakes and, in the process, created the Niagara Escarpment—a prominent geological formation that plays a crucial role in the formation of the falls. The unique topography of the region, with its cliffs and gorges, set the stage for the breathtaking spectacle we witness today.

Indigenous peoples, including the Haudenosaunee (Iroquois) and the Neutral Nation, were among the first inhabitants of the Niagara region. For these communities, the falls held significant spiritual and cultural importance. The Haudenosaunee, in particular, referred to the falls as "Onguiaahra," meaning "The Strait."

The arrival of European explorers in the 17th century brought a new chapter to Niagara's history. French explorer Samuel de Champlain was one of the first Europeans to document the falls in 1604. As the fur trade flourished, Niagara became a strategic area for European powers vying for control of North America.

In the 19th century, the construction of the Erie Canal and the Welland Canal transformed Niagara into a key transportation hub. The increasing industrialization brought economic prosperity to the region but also raised concerns about environmental conservation. Visionaries like Frederick Law Olmsted, the landscape architect famous for designing Central Park, played a crucial role in advocating for the preservation of Niagara's natural beauty.

The mid-19th century also saw the advent of tourism around Niagara Falls. The completion of the first suspension bridge over the Niagara River in 1848 made the falls more accessible, attracting visitors eager to witness the awe-inspiring sight. The burgeoning tourism industry led to the development of hotels, attractions, and the establishment of parks around the falls.

Niagara Falls gained international attention during the 20th century, not only for its natural beauty but also for daredevils who attempted daring feats. Names like Annie Edson Taylor, the first person to go over the falls in a barrel and survive, became synonymous with the adventurous spirit of Niagara.

The conservation efforts intensified in the 20th century, leading to the creation of the Niagara Reservation State Park—the oldest state park in the United States—in 1885. The park aimed to preserve the natural surroundings of the falls and provide public access for generations to come.

Today, Niagara Falls continues to be a symbol of natural grandeur, drawing millions of visitors each year. The falls' history is not just a chronicle of geological processes but a testament to the enduring relationship between humanity and nature—a relationship that has evolved over millennia and continues to captivate those who stand on the shores, gazing at the powerful and timeless beauty of Niagara Falls.

Chapter 2: Getting Ready for Adventure

Packing Essentials

Packing for a trip to the mesmerizing Niagara Falls requires careful consideration to ensure you're well-prepared for a range of activities and weather conditions. Whether you're an adventure seeker or a leisure traveler, having the right essentials can make your experience even more enjoyable.

Clothing:

Weather-Appropriate Attire:
Given the variable weather, pack layers. Comfortable jeans or pants and T-shirts are great for the day, while a light jacket or sweater can come in handy in the evenings.

Waterproof Outerwear:
The falls generate a mist that can leave you damp. A waterproof jacket or poncho ensures you stay dry during close encounters with the cascading waters.

Comfortable Footwear:
You'll likely be doing a fair amount of walking, so comfortable, waterproof shoes are essential. If you plan on hiking, consider sturdy hiking boots.

Accessories:

Water-Resistant Accessories:
Protect your electronics and important documents with water-resistant pouches or bags. This is especially crucial during boat tours.

Sun Protection:
Niagara can be sunny, so pack sunglasses, a wide-brimmed hat, and sunscreen to shield yourself from UV rays.

Camera and Binoculars:
Capture the breathtaking scenery with a good camera. Binoculars can also enhance your experience, allowing you to see details that might be missed with the naked eye.

Practical Items:

Power Bank:
Ensure your devices stay charged, especially if you're relying on them for navigation or capturing memories.

Reusable Water Bottle:
Staying hydrated is key. Bring a reusable water bottle to refill throughout the day.

Snacks:
Pack some energy-boosting snacks to keep you fueled during your adventures. Granola bars, nuts, and dried fruits are convenient options.

Travel Documents:

Identification and Travel Insurance:
Carry a valid ID, and if you're an international traveler, ensure you have your passport. Travel insurance is also recommended for unforeseen circumstances.

Reservations and Itinerary:
Print or have electronic copies of your hotel reservations, tour bookings, and a general itinerary. This can be helpful for reference.

Health and Safety:

First Aid Kit:
A basic first aid kit with bandages, pain relievers, and any personal medications is essential for unexpected situations.

Insect Repellent:
If you plan on exploring nature trails or parks, insect repellent can protect you from mosquitoes.

Emergency Contact Information:
Have a list of emergency contacts, including local authorities, in case of any unforeseen incidents.

By packing these essentials, you'll be well-prepared to embrace the wonders of Niagara Falls while staying comfortable and safe throughout your journey. Remember, the key is to strike a balance between preparedness and the joy of spontaneity that travel often brings.

Best Times to Visit

Planning your visit to Niagara Falls requires careful consideration of the weather, crowd levels, and the overall experience you're seeking. The iconic falls offer a different charm each season, providing visitors with unique perspectives and activities. Here's a guide to help you decide on the best times to experience Niagara Falls at its finest.

Spring (April to June):
Spring is a wonderful time to visit Niagara Falls. The weather is mild, and the surrounding landscape comes to life with blossoming flowers and vibrant greenery. The mist from the falls, coupled with the warm temperatures, creates a refreshing and invigorating atmosphere. The crowds are relatively smaller compared to the peak summer season, allowing for a more intimate experience with the natural

beauty of the falls. Consider late spring for the best balance between favorable weather and fewer tourists.

Summer (July to August):
Summer is undoubtedly the peak tourist season at Niagara Falls. The weather is warm, and the falls are surrounded by lush greenery. This is the time for boat tours, outdoor activities, and vibrant evening illuminations. However, be prepared for larger crowds and longer wait times for popular attractions. To make the most of your summer visit, plan to arrive early in the day or later in the evening to avoid the busiest times.

Fall (September to November):
Fall brings a spectacular display of colors to the Niagara region as the foliage transforms into a stunning palette of red, orange, and gold. The weather remains pleasant, making it an excellent time for hiking and exploring the scenic surroundings. While the crowds start to thin out after summer, it's advisable to check for local events, as fall foliage can attract visitors seeking the beauty of autumn.

Winter (December to March):
Winter adds a magical touch to Niagara Falls as the mist from the falls creates a frosty wonderland. While some attractions may close during the winter months, the icy spectacle of the falls is a sight to behold. Winter also offers unique activities such as ice skating near the falls and the Winter Festival of Lights, where the falls are illuminated with colorful lights. If you don't mind the cold, winter provides a serene and enchanting experience.

Choosing the best time to visit Niagara Falls depends on your preferences and the kind of experience you're looking for. Whether it's the vibrant colors of fall, the refreshing mist of spring, the bustling energy of summer, or the icy beauty of winter, Niagara Falls has something incredible to offer year-round. Consider the season that aligns with your interests and get ready for an unforgettable adventure at one of the world's most awe-inspiring natural wonders.

Navigating the Area

Navigating the Niagara Falls region requires a blend of strategic planning and spontaneous exploration. The area, known for its captivating beauty and diverse attractions, offers a multitude of transportation options and pathways for an unforgettable adventure.

Transportation Hubs

Niagara Falls is well-connected by various transportation modes, making it accessible for travelers from different corners of the globe. If you're arriving by air, the nearest major airport is Buffalo Niagara International Airport, located about 30 minutes away. Alternatively, Toronto Pearson International Airport is approximately 90 minutes away, offering a convenient gateway for international visitors.

Once you've landed, ground transportation options abound. Shuttle services, taxis, and rental cars are readily available, providing a seamless transition from the airport to your desired destination. For those looking to add a touch of luxury to their journey, consider hiring a limousine service, which not only offers comfort but also panoramic views of the surrounding landscapes.

Exploring on Foot

One of the best ways to truly absorb the magic of Niagara Falls is by exploring on foot. The town itself is pedestrian-friendly, with well-maintained sidewalks and walking paths.

Stroll along the Niagara Parkway, a scenic route that runs parallel to the river and offers breathtaking views of the falls. This leisurely walk allows you to take in the natural beauty at your own pace, with plenty of opportunities to stop and capture the perfect photo.

Cruise the River

Navigating the area isn't limited to the land. Experience the sheer power and grandeur of Niagara Falls by taking a boat tour. The iconic Maid of the Mist boat cruise takes you up close and personal with the falls, providing an immersive experience that you'll remember for a lifetime. Don a waterproof poncho and feel the mist on your face as you sail into the heart of the cascading waters—an adventure that adds a thrill to your exploration.

Hop-On, Hop-Off Buses

For a more comprehensive tour of the region, consider utilizing the hop-on, hop-off bus services. These double-decker buses provide a convenient and flexible way to explore the various attractions in and around Niagara Falls. With designated stops at key points of interest, you can tailor your journey to match your interests. Whether you want to visit the botanical gardens, explore historical sites, or indulge in a shopping spree, these buses offer a hassle-free way to navigate the area.

Biking Adventures

For the more adventurous souls, renting a bike opens up a world of possibilities. Several bike rental services operate in the area, offering a chance to traverse the Niagara Parkway's scenic trails. Biking not only provides an eco-friendly mode of transportation but also allows you to cover more ground and discover hidden gems that might be missed by other means.

Navigating the Niagara Falls area is an integral part of the overall experience. From traditional modes of transportation to exhilarating boat cruises and leisurely walks, the options are as diverse as the attractions themselves. Whether you choose to explore on foot, by bus, or via the water, the journey through this mesmerizing region is bound to be as memorable as the destination itself.

Chapter 3: The Majestic Niagara Falls

Up-Close with the Falls

Standing at the edge of Niagara Falls is a breathtaking experience that transcends the ordinary. As you approach the falls, the thunderous roar becomes a symphony, echoing the raw power and beauty of nature. In this chapter, we explore the myriad ways to get up-close and personal with one of the world's most iconic natural wonders.

Maid of the Mist: A Voyage into the Misty Abyss

One of the quintessential Niagara Falls experiences is the Maid of the Mist boat tour. As you board the iconic blue poncho-clad boat, you embark on a journey that takes you within arm's reach of the awe-inspiring Horseshoe Falls. The mist rises like ethereal spirits, enveloping you in a cool embrace. The sound of rushing water becomes a thunderous applause, a testament to the sheer force of nature.

The Maid of the Mist adventure isn't just a visual spectacle; it's a sensory immersion. The vibrations of the falls resonate through the boat, creating an almost primal connection with the elemental forces at play. Rainbows dance in the mist, casting a spectrum of colors that adds a touch of magic to the experience.

Journey Behind the Falls: Behind the Veil

For those seeking a different perspective, the Journey Behind the Falls offers a unique vantage point. An elevator descends through solid rock to tunnels that lead you to portals directly behind the falls. As you step onto the observation deck, you find yourself mere feet away from the rushing water, separated only by a sheet of mist and a thin layer of rock.

The sensation is both humbling and exhilarating. You can feel the vibrations of the falls reverberating through the rock, creating an immersive encounter with the elemental forces. The observation deck allows for uninterrupted views, providing a rare glimpse into the heart of the falls. The sheer power of the water is palpable, a reminder of nature's untamed beauty.

Capturing the Perfect Photo: Tips for Photographers

For photography enthusiasts, capturing the essence of Niagara Falls up-close is both a challenge and a delight. The ever-present mist adds an ethereal quality to the scene, but it requires some finesse to protect your equipment. Consider bringing a waterproof cover for your camera and experimenting with different exposure settings to capture the dynamic range of the falls.

Timing is crucial. The play of light during sunrise or sunset can transform the falls into a cascade of golden hues. Additionally, visiting during the off-peak seasons allows for a more intimate experience, with fewer crowds vying for the perfect shot.

Getting up-close with Niagara Falls is an adventure for the senses. Whether you choose the immersive Maid of the Mist, the contemplative Journey Behind the Falls, or aim to capture the perfect photo, each approach offers a unique perspective on the raw power and beauty of this natural wonder. It's a moment that lingers in your memory, a testament to the timeless allure of Niagara Falls.

Behind the Scenes: Tours and Facts

Delving into the heart of Niagara Falls goes beyond the awe-inspiring view from the observation decks. This chapter takes you behind the scenes, offering exclusive tours and uncovering fascinating facts that add a layer of intrigue to the natural wonder.

Tours Beyond the Edge:

Maid of the Mist VIP Experience:
Beyond the classic Maid of the Mist boat tour, there's a VIP experience that takes you closer than ever to the roaring falls. Don a poncho and embark on a journey that not only provides a thrilling encounter with the cascading waters but also offers insights from expert guides. Learn about the geological history and the tales of daredevils who attempted daring feats over the falls.

Cave of the Winds Tour:
Feel the power of the falls up close with the Cave of the Winds tour. Journey down to the base of Bridal Veil Falls, navigating through wooden walkways. The hurricane deck experience brings you within arm's reach of the thundering waters. Guides share geological marvels and stories of the falls' formation, providing a sensory adventure unlike any other.

Fascinating Facts:

The Geological Tapestry:
Niagara Falls isn't just a stunning visual spectacle; it's a geological masterpiece. Unravel the story of how glaciers shaped the landscape thousands of years ago, carving out the Niagara Gorge and leaving behind this breathtaking natural wonder. Discover the layers of rock that tell a tale of ancient times, adding a deep sense of history to your experience.

The Seasonal Symphony:
Niagara Falls undergoes a transformative journey with each season. In winter, witness the falls adorned in an icy cloak, while spring brings a surge in water flow. Summer showcases the falls in all their glory, and fall paints the landscape with a vibrant palette. Tours provide a front-row seat to this seasonal symphony, allowing you to appreciate the ever-changing beauty of the falls.

The Daredevils' Legacy:
Niagara Falls has a history peppered with daredevils who braved the currents for fame and adventure. Hear tales of those who tightrope-walked across the falls or went over them in barrels. Explore the spots where these daring feats took place, and gain a newfound respect for the courageous individuals who left an indelible mark on Niagara's history.
Conservation Efforts:

Peek behind the curtain to understand the ongoing conservation efforts dedicated to preserving the falls for future generations. Learn about sustainable tourism practices, habitat preservation, and water quality initiatives. Tours highlight the importance of environmental stewardship, inviting visitors to be part of the mission to protect this natural wonder.

Embarking on the behind-the-scenes tours and immersing yourself in the facts surrounding Niagara Falls adds depth to your journey. It transforms your visit from a mere sightseeing adventure into an educational and awe-inspiring experience, leaving you with a profound appreciation for the falls' natural and historical significance.

Capturing the Perfect Photo

In the realm of Niagara Falls, where nature's grandeur meets human fascination, the pursuit of the perfect photograph becomes a quest of its own. Chapter 3.3 delves into the art and science of capturing the essence of the falls through the lens. From strategic vantage points to the play of light and water, here's your guide to immortalizing Niagara's beauty in a frame.

Understanding the Elements

Photographing Niagara Falls requires an understanding of the natural elements at play. The mist rising from the cascade adds an ethereal quality to the scene but can be a challenge for your equipment. Ensure your camera gear is protected against water droplets, and consider using a lens hood to shield your lens.

The dynamic nature of the falls demands versatility in your camera settings. Experiment with different shutter speeds to either freeze the motion of the water or create a dreamy, flowing effect. A tripod can be your best ally in achieving the desired stability for those long exposure shots.

Timing is Everything

To truly capture the magic of Niagara Falls, timing is crucial. The falls undergo a breathtaking transformation at different times of the day. Early mornings often provide a serene atmosphere with soft, golden light, while late afternoons showcase the falls in a warm glow. Sunset, with its vibrant hues, can turn the scene into a painter's palette. For a unique perspective, try capturing the falls during the misty dawn or under the enchanting moonlight.

Strategic Vantage Points

Niagara offers a multitude of vantage points, each providing a distinct view of the falls. Journey behind the falls for an up-close and personal experience, capturing the raw power from a unique angle. The observation decks on both the American and Canadian sides offer panoramic views, allowing you to frame the falls against the backdrop of the surrounding landscape.

Consider taking a boat tour, such as the iconic Maid of the Mist, for a water-level perspective. These journeys not only provide an exhilarating experience but also open up new photographic opportunities. The juxtaposition of the boat against the mighty falls can add a dynamic element to your shots.

Composition Techniques

Beyond the technical aspects, the composition is key to creating a compelling photograph. Use foreground elements, such as rocks or vegetation, to add depth to your shots. Experiment with different angles to find the most captivating composition. Including people in your photos can provide a sense of scale and convey the sheer magnitude of the falls.

Don't shy away from capturing the details—the delicate flowers in the nearby gardens, the intricate patterns in the mist, or the play of light on the water's surface. These details can add a layer of complexity and nuance to your photographic narrative.

Post-Processing Magic

Once you've captured the raw beauty of Niagara Falls, post-processing can elevate your photographs to new heights. Adjustments to contrast, saturation, and sharpness can enhance the visual impact. Experiment with black and white conversions to evoke a timeless, classic feel.

Remember, the perfect photo is not just about technical perfection but about conveying the emotions stirred by this natural wonder. Let your creativity flow, and let the falls be your muse as you embark on the journey to capture the perfect photograph.

Chapter 4: On the Water

Maid of the Mist: A Classic Experience

One cannot truly claim to have experienced Niagara Falls without embarking on the iconic Maid of the Mist boat tour. This classic adventure has been delighting visitors for well over a century, offering an up-close and personal encounter with the thundering majesty of the falls.

A Journey into the Mist

As you step onto the Maid of the Mist boat, you can feel the anticipation building. The roar of the falls grows louder as the boat navigates the waters, taking you closer to the heart of this natural wonder. The first sight of the American and Horseshoe Falls from the deck is nothing short of awe-inspiring.

The Blue Poncho Tradition

Upon boarding, visitors are handed the signature blue Maid of the Mist poncho. This isn't just a practical accessory; it's a rite of passage. The mist from the falls creates a mesmerizing spectacle, and the poncho is your shield as you sail into the heart of the mist. It's not just a garment; it's a symbol of the immersive experience that awaits.

Capturing the Perfect Shot

As the boat inches closer to the falls, the sheer power and beauty of the cascading water become apparent. This is a photographer's dream. The mist creates an ethereal atmosphere, and rainbows often dance in the spray. Be sure to have your camera ready as you're guaranteed to capture breathtaking shots that will become cherished memories.

A Historical Perspective

The Maid of the Mist has a rich history dating back to 1846 when it began as a ferry service. Over the years, it has evolved into the world-famous attraction it is today. Riding the Maid of the Mist is not just a thrilling experience; it's a journey through time, connecting you with the countless adventurers who have marveled at Niagara's grandeur before you.

Seasonal Delights

The Maid of the Mist operates from late April to early November, allowing visitors to witness the falls in different seasons. Spring brings a rush of water from the melting snow, while summer offers a lush, green backdrop. In the fall, the surrounding foliage transforms into a riot of colors, providing a unique perspective of this natural masterpiece.

Family-Friendly Adventure

The Maid of the Mist is a family-friendly adventure suitable for all ages. The excitement on the faces of children as they feel the mist and witness the falls up close is priceless. It's an educational experience wrapped in exhilaration, making it a must-do for families visiting Niagara.

Beyond the Boat Ride

The Maid of the Mist experience doesn't end when the boat docks. Visitors can explore the surrounding area, visit the observation decks, and learn more about the geological and historical significance of Niagara Falls. The memories created on the Maid of the Mist linger long after the boat ride is over.

In essence, the Maid of the Mist is not merely a boat tour; it's a journey into the heart of Niagara Falls. It's a sensory adventure that leaves an indelible mark on all who have the privilege of experiencing it—a classic, timeless encounter with the raw power and beauty of nature.

Jet Boating Thrills

When it comes to experiencing the raw power and majesty of Niagara Falls up close, few adventures compare to the exhilarating thrills of jet boating. This chapter is all about embracing the adrenaline-pumping experience of jet boating near the falls, where the combination of speed, water, and the breathtaking surroundings creates an unforgettable adventure.

The Ride of a Lifetime

Imagine being aboard a high-speed jet boat, racing across the churning waters of the Niagara River towards the iconic falls. As the boat accelerates, you can feel the rush of wind against your face and the mist from the falls spraying around you. Jet boating offers an unmatched, heart-pounding adventure that brings you as close as safely possible to the powerful cascades.

Choosing Your Adventure

Several jet boat tour operators provide different experiences tailored to various levels of thrill-seekers. Whether you're a first-timer seeking a taste of excitement or an adrenaline junkie craving an intense ride, there's a jet boating adventure for everyone. Tours typically range from mild to wild, with skilled captains navigating through the turbulent waters, providing both safety and an adrenaline rush.

Safety First, Thrills Second

Before embarking on your jet boating adventure, safety briefings are conducted to ensure everyone understands the importance of following guidelines. Passengers are provided with waterproof gear to protect against the inevitable splashes from the river. The tour operators prioritize safety without compromising the excitement, making it an accessible adventure for all thrill enthusiasts.

Views Like Never Before

The vantage point from a jet boat is unique, offering perspectives of Niagara Falls that few get to witness. As you approach the falls, you can feel the intensity of the water, hear the thunderous roar, and witness the mist rising like ethereal clouds. The boat maneuvers skillfully, providing ample opportunities for passengers to capture these awe-inspiring moments with their cameras.

Beyond the Falls

While the highlight of the jet boat tour is undoubtedly the proximity to Niagara Falls, the adventure doesn't end there. The tour often includes exploration of the scenic Niagara Gorge, where you can marvel at the geological wonders and lush landscapes that surround the river. The guides share fascinating insights into the history, geology, and ecology of the area, enhancing the overall experience.

Tips for Jet Boating Success

For those gearing up for a jet boating adventure, it's essential to wear comfortable clothing and secure any personal items to prevent them from being lost during the ride. Bringing a waterproof camera or smartphone is also recommended to capture the thrilling moments without worrying about water damage.

Jet boating near Niagara Falls is not just an adventure; it's an immersive and thrilling journey into the heart of one of nature's most spectacular wonders. Whether you're a daredevil seeking an adrenaline rush or someone looking to experience the falls in a unique way, jet boating promises an unforgettable ride on the wild waters of the Niagara River. Strap in, hold on tight, and get ready for an adventure of a lifetime!

Exploring the Islands

Niagara Falls isn't just about the majestic falls; it's also about the hidden gems that lie within the river. The islands surrounding the falls offer a unique and enchanting perspective, providing visitors with an opportunity to experience nature in its unspoiled beauty.

Discovering Paradise Islands

As you embark on the journey to explore the islands near Niagara Falls, one name stands out – Paradise Island. Accessible by boat, this serene retreat offers a haven for nature enthusiasts. The lush greenery and the sounds of the rushing river create a tranquil atmosphere, a stark contrast to the thunderous roar of the falls. It's a perfect spot for a leisurely hike or a peaceful picnic surrounded by the symphony of nature.

Three Sisters Islands: A Trilogy of Beauty

Named after the three daughters of General Parkhurst Whitney, Three Sisters Islands present a trilogy of beauty in the Niagara River. Connected by bridges, these islands offer stunning views of the American Falls. The walking paths winding through the islands provide an intimate experience with the rushing waters. It's a photographer's dream, capturing the raw power of the falls from unique vantage points.

Luna Island: Up Close with Bridal Veil Falls

For those seeking an up-close encounter with Bridal Veil Falls, Luna Island is the place to be. Positioned between the American Falls and Bridal Veil Falls, this tiny island provides an immersive experience. Walk along the boardwalk and feel the mist on your face as you stand just a stone's throw away from the cascading waters. Luna Island offers a sensory journey, allowing you to touch, see, and hear the falls in a way that's impossible from the mainland.

Goat Island: Nature's Playground

The largest island on the Niagara River, Goat Island, is a playground of nature's wonders. Accessible by bridge from the American mainland, this island is a haven for adventurers. Trails meander through ancient landscapes, providing glimpses of wildlife and breathtaking vistas of the falls. The Cave of the Winds attraction on Goat Island takes you to the very base of the falls, where you can feel the full force of the water.

Navigating the Islands

To explore these islands, various guided tours and boat excursions are available. Whether you choose a peaceful kayak journey or an exhilarating jet boat ride, each option offers a different perspective on the islands and the falls. Many tour operators provide insightful commentary, sharing the rich history and ecological importance of these natural wonders.

Exploring the islands around Niagara Falls is a journey into the heart of nature's grandeur. From the tranquility of Paradise Island to the up-close encounters on Luna Island, each spot offers a unique experience. These islands are not just geographical features; they are integral parts of the Niagara Falls story, adding layers of beauty and adventure to an already mesmerizing destination. So, put on your explorer's hat and get ready to uncover the secrets that the islands of Niagara Falls hold.

Chapter 5: Land Adventures

Hiking Trails with a View

Niagara Falls isn't just about the cascading water—it's also a haven for hiking enthusiasts seeking a unique perspective of this natural wonder. Lace up your hiking boots and get ready to be mesmerized by the beauty that unfolds along these scenic trails.

1. Niagara Glen Nature Centre Trail:
Begin your adventure at the Niagara Glen Nature Centre, where a trail network awaits, offering some of the most spectacular views of the Niagara River Whirlpool. The trail winds through a lush Carolinian forest, and as you ascend, the roar of the falls grows distant, replaced by the soothing sounds of nature. Keep an eye out for unique flora and fauna that call this gorge home.

2. Bruce Trail - Niagara Section:
As part of the renowned Bruce Trail, the Niagara section takes hikers through a diverse landscape, including lush forests, meadows, and along the edge of the Niagara Escarpment. The viewpoints along this trail provide sweeping panoramas of both the Canadian and American falls. It's a hiker's paradise, offering varying difficulty levels to cater to all adventure seekers.

3. Whirlpool Rapids Trail:
For those seeking a trail that combines natural beauty with a bit of excitement, the Whirlpool Rapids Trail is a perfect choice. The trail follows the Niagara River and offers vantage points to witness the mesmerizing rapids. The energy and power of the rushing waters are truly awe-inspiring.

4. Devil's Hole State Park Trail:
Venture into the heart of Devil's Hole State Park for a trail that offers not only scenic views but also a glimpse into the region's history. The trail takes you along the Niagara Gorge, with views of the rapids and whirlpool. Explore the captivating geological formations and learn about the area's fascinating past.

5. Dufferin Islands Nature Area:
Escape the bustling crowds and immerse yourself in the tranquility of Dufferin Islands Nature Area. This oasis of calmness features a network of trails surrounded by lush greenery and peaceful lagoons. The trails wind around the islands, providing a serene setting to enjoy the natural beauty away from the rush of the falls.

Whether you're an avid hiker or a casual nature enthusiast, these trails offer a perfect blend of adventure and tranquility. Each step brings you closer to not just the falls, but to the heart of the natural wonders that make Niagara a destination like no other. So, pack your sense of adventure and get ready to experience the awe-inspiring beauty that awaits along these hiking trails with unparalleled views of Niagara Falls.

Biking Around the Falls

When it comes to exploring the breathtaking beauty of Niagara Falls and its surrounding areas, few experiences match the freedom and exhilaration of biking. Cycling not only allows you to cover more ground but also lets you immerse yourself in the sights and sounds of this natural wonder at your own pace.

Unveiling the Trails

Niagara Falls boasts a network of scenic biking trails that cater to all skill levels, from casual riders to avid cyclists seeking a challenge. One of the most popular routes is the Niagara River Recreation Trail, stretching approximately 35 miles from Fort Erie to Niagara-on-the-Lake. This trail offers a front-row seat to the mesmerizing views of the Niagara River, with the falls as a constant companion.

For those looking for a more off-the-beaten-path adventure, the Greater Niagara Circle Route takes you on a 140-kilometer loop, guiding you through quaint towns, vineyards, and hidden gems. This route provides a unique perspective of the falls while allowing you to explore the diverse landscapes that make up the Niagara region.

Two-Wheeled Thrills

As you pedal along the designated biking paths, you'll feel the cool mist from the falls on your face and hear the roaring water as a constant soundtrack. Biking provides a sense of intimacy with nature that other modes of transportation may not offer. Whether you choose a leisurely ride or a more challenging route, the experience of the wind in your hair and the scent of the surrounding foliage is unparalleled.

For those seeking an adrenaline rush, consider venturing onto the Niagara Gorge Rim Trail. This trail takes you closer to the edge, offering heart-pounding views of the gorge and the falls. It's a ride for the daring, with twists and turns that keep you on the edge of your saddle.

Pit Stops and Picnics

Biking around the falls isn't just about the journey; it's also about the delightful pit stops along the way. Numerous parks and lookout points invite you to take a break, soak in the scenery, and capture Instagram-worthy photos. Pack a picnic and stop at Dufferin Islands for a serene lunch amidst the lush greenery, or head to Queen Victoria Park for a view of the falls that will leave you breathless.

Local vendors and cafes line the biking trails, offering refreshing treats and snacks to fuel your adventure. From ice cream stands with a view to quaint coffee shops tucked away in the towns, each stop adds a flavorful touch to your biking experience.

Practical Tips for Biking Bliss

Before embarking on your biking escapade, ensure you have the right equipment. Local rental shops provide a variety of bikes suitable for different terrains. Helmets, maps, and insider tips on the best routes are often included in rental packages.

Check the weather forecast, wear comfortable clothing, and bring a water bottle to stay hydrated. Don't forget your camera; you'll want to capture the memories of your two-wheeled journey around one of the world's most iconic natural wonders.

Biking around Niagara Falls offers a unique blend of adventure, natural beauty, and the freedom to chart your course. Whether you're an avid cyclist or a casual rider, the experience of pedaling along the scenic trails, feeling the mist on your face, and taking in the awe-inspiring sights of the falls is bound to be a highlight of your Niagara adventure. So, grab a bike, hit the trails, and let the beauty of Niagara unfold before you with every turn of the pedal.

Zip-lining Over the Gorge

Zip-lining over the Niagara Gorge is not just an adventure; it's a heart-pounding, adrenaline-pumping experience that will leave you breathless and craving for more. This unique activity takes the concept of sightseeing to a whole new level, offering an exhilarating journey with panoramic views of the breathtaking Niagara Falls and the rugged gorge below.

Soaring Across the Sky

As you step up to the launch platform, anticipation and excitement build. The harness is snug, the helmet secure—your adventure is about to begin. The first few steps onto the platform might be nerve-wracking, but as you glide along the zip line, any initial apprehension transforms into sheer awe. The feeling of soaring through the air, with the mist of the falls on your face, is indescribable.

Unparalleled Views

The zip-line route provides unparalleled views of the Niagara River and the magnificent Horseshoe Falls. As you zip across the gorge, you'll witness the water below in its untamed glory, carving its way through the rocky landscape. The sheer power and force of nature become palpable, making this not just a thrilling ride but a visual feast for the senses.

A Symphony of Senses

The sound of rushing water, the cool breeze against your face, and the sight of the mist rising from the falls create a symphony of sensations. It's a moment where time seems to stand still, allowing you to fully immerse yourself in the grandeur of the surroundings. Zip-lining over the gorge offers a unique perspective, showcasing the natural beauty of the area from a vantage point few get to experience.

Safety and Expert Guidance

Safety is, of course, a top priority. Before taking flight, experienced guides provide thorough instructions on the equipment and the do's and don'ts. The state-of-the-art zip-lining gear ensures a secure and comfortable ride. Trained professionals are with you every step of the way, ensuring not only your safety but also enhancing the overall experience with their knowledge and anecdotes about the gorge's geological wonders.

An Adventure for All

Zip-lining over the gorge is not limited to the adrenaline junkies; it's an adventure accessible to a wide range of ages and fitness levels. Whether you're a thrill-seeker looking for the next big rush or a family seeking a memorable experience together, this activity caters to various preferences.

Capturing the Moment

Don't forget to capture the moment. Many zip-lining experiences offer the option to have photos or videos taken during your flight. Imagine having a memento of yourself soaring above the Niagara Gorge, with the falls as your backdrop—a memory to share and cherish for years to come.

Zip-lining over the gorge is a must-try for anyone visiting Niagara Falls. It's not just an adventure activity; it's a journey into the heart of nature's magnificence, a chance to feel the pulse of the falls and the energy of the gorge. So, gear up, take that leap, and let the thrill of zip-lining become a highlight of your Niagara adventure.

Chapter 6: Entertainment Beyond the Falls

Clifton Hill: The Entertainment Hub

Niagara Falls is not just about the breathtaking cascade of water—it's also about the vibrant energy that surrounds it. One place that encapsulates the sheer exuberance and fun that the area has to offer is Clifton Hill, often dubbed as the Entertainment Hub of Niagara Falls.

Clifton Hill Unveiled

At the heart of Niagara's tourist district, Clifton Hill stands as a bustling promenade that welcomes visitors with a kaleidoscope of lights, sounds, and activities. This lively street is a haven for those seeking a mix of family-friendly amusements, thrilling adventures, and a dash of nostalgia.

The Neon Wonderland

As the sun sets and the Falls are illuminated, Clifton Hill comes alive with a neon glow. The street is lined with a dazzling array of attractions, including arcades, haunted houses, and amusement centers. The vibrant colors and flashing lights create an enchanting atmosphere that's irresistible to both kids and adults alike.

Arcades Galore

One of the highlights of Clifton Hill is its collection of arcades that evoke the golden age of gaming. From classic pinball machines to the latest virtual reality experiences, these arcades cater to all generations of gamers. The sound of bells and whistles mingles with laughter as families engage in friendly competition, creating an atmosphere of pure joy.

Haunted Houses and Thrill Rides

For those seeking an adrenaline rush, Clifton Hill doesn't disappoint. The street is home to several haunted houses and thrilling rides that promise to send shivers down your spine. The spine-tingling experiences are not just limited to Halloween; these attractions operate year-round, adding an extra layer of excitement to any visit.

Culinary Delights

Clifton Hill is not just about thrills and chills—it's also a food lover's paradise. The street is dotted with a variety of restaurants and cafes serving everything from classic comfort food to international cuisine. Whether you're craving a hearty burger, indulgent desserts, or a quick snack to fuel your adventures, Clifton Hill has you covered.

Nostalgic Charm

Beyond the modern attractions, Clifton Hill preserves a touch of nostalgia. Classic establishments like the Great Canadian Midway, with its colorful Ferris wheel, and the Movieland Wax Museum, take visitors on a journey back in time. The iconic SkyWheel offers panoramic views of the Falls and the surrounding landscape, creating lasting memories for those who dare to take a ride.

Family-Friendly Atmosphere

What sets Clifton Hill apart is its commitment to providing a family-friendly environment. The street is designed to cater to visitors of all ages, ensuring that everyone can partake in the joy and excitement. The laughter of children, the camaraderie of friends, and the shared moments of amazement make Clifton Hill a place where memories are created and cherished.

In essence, Clifton Hill is more than a collection of attractions—it's a celebration of the spirit of Niagara Falls. As you stroll down this iconic street, you'll find yourself immersed in a world where fun knows no bounds, and every step is a new adventure. Whether you're a thrill-seeker, a gaming enthusiast, or a family looking for quality time, Clifton Hill is the quintessential Entertainment Hub that encapsulates the magic of Niagara Falls.

Casino Nights

Niagara Falls is not only about the awe-inspiring natural wonder but also about the pulsating energy of the vibrant entertainment scene. One of the most exciting aspects of the nightlife is the allure of Casino Nights. As the sun sets and the falls are illuminated, the casinos come to life, offering a unique blend of glamour, excitement, and a bit of luck.
The Glittering Casinos

Niagara Falls boasts several world-class casinos, each with its own charm and offerings. The most iconic among them is the Fallsview Casino Resort. Perched overlooking the Horseshoe Falls, this sprawling complex is not only a gambler's paradise but also a visual feast with its stunning views. The vibrant colors of the casino lights reflecting off the cascading water create a magical atmosphere that sets the stage for a night of indulgence.

Gaming Extravaganza

Step inside the casino, and you'll be greeted by the unmistakable sounds of slot machines chiming and cards shuffling. The gaming floor is a mosaic of excitement, with tables for classic games like blackjack, poker, roulette, and more. Whether you're a seasoned gambler or a novice trying your luck, the friendly and professional dealers make the experience enjoyable for everyone.

Entertainment Beyond Gambling

Casino Nights at Niagara Falls are not just about testing your luck on the tables. These establishments are full-fledged entertainment hubs. Many casinos host live performances, concerts, and comedy shows, adding an extra layer of excitement to your evening. Imagine enjoying a world-class performance after a thrilling round of blackjack, with the falls as your backdrop—truly an unforgettable experience.

Gourmet Indulgence

Feeling peckish after a round of games? Niagara Falls casinos are home to some of the finest dining establishments. From upscale restaurants with panoramic views of the falls to casual eateries offering diverse cuisines, there's something to satisfy every palate. It's not just about winning at the tables; it's about savoring the finest flavors the region has to offer.

Nightlife Unleashed

As the night progresses, the energy in the casinos reaches its peak. The vibrant nightlife spills out from the gaming floors to the bars and lounges within the establishments. Sip on a signature cocktail crafted by expert mixologists while taking in the lively atmosphere. The casino nightlife is a perfect blend of sophistication and revelry, making it an ideal setting for celebrations or simply a memorable night out.

Tips for a Stellar Casino Night

For those new to the casino scene, a few tips can enhance your experience. Set a budget for the night, savor the games without feeling pressured to win big, and most importantly, relish the overall ambiance. Whether you're celebrating a special occasion or just looking for a thrilling night out, Casino Nights at Niagara Falls promise an experience that goes beyond the ordinary.

In the heart of this entertainment haven, under the vibrant lights and beside one of the world's greatest natural wonders, Casino Nights at Niagara Falls beckon you to try your luck and create memories that will last a lifetime. So, roll the dice, shuffle the cards, and let the night unfold in the enchanting glow of the falls.

Festivals and Events

Niagara Falls isn't just a breathtaking natural wonder; it's also a hub of vibrant festivals and events that add an extra layer of excitement to your visit. Throughout the year, the region comes alive with celebrations that cater to a variety of interests. Here's a glimpse into the kaleidoscope of festivals and events you can experience around Niagara Falls.

1. ** Niagara Falls Winter Festival of Lights

As the winter chill sets in, Niagara Falls transforms into a dazzling winter wonderland during the Winter Festival of Lights. Millions of sparkling lights illuminate the falls, creating a mesmerizing visual spectacle. The festival also features fireworks, interactive light displays, and various activities for visitors of all ages. It's a magical way to experience the beauty of the falls in a completely different light.

2. Niagara Food and Wine Festival

For the culinary enthusiasts, the Niagara Food and Wine Festival is a must-attend event. Held annually, this festival showcases the region's finest wines, local produce, and culinary talents. Visitors can indulge in wine tastings, gourmet dinners, and cooking demonstrations. The backdrop of Niagara Falls adds a touch of elegance to this gastronomic celebration.

3. Niagara Falls International Marathon

Fitness enthusiasts and running aficionados gather for the Niagara Falls International Marathon, a scenic race that takes participants through the stunning landscapes surrounding the falls. Whether you're a seasoned marathoner or a casual runner, the breathtaking views along the route make this event a unique and memorable experience.

4. Niagara Falls Music Festivals

Music lovers rejoice during various music festivals held in the Niagara region. From jazz and blues to contemporary and classical, these festivals cater to diverse musical tastes. Imagine enjoying a live performance with the iconic falls as a backdrop, creating an unforgettable symphony of sound and nature.

5. Niagara Falls Elvis Festival

Step back in time and celebrate the King of Rock 'n' Roll at the Niagara Falls Elvis Festival. This annual event brings together Elvis tribute artists from around the world, competing for the title of the best Elvis impersonator. The energy and excitement of this festival are contagious, making it a unique and entertaining experience for fans of all ages.

6. Niagara Falls Comic Con

Embrace your inner geek at the Niagara Falls Comic Con, where pop culture, comics, and fandom collide. This event attracts fans, cosplayers, and celebrities, creating a lively atmosphere filled with creativity and passion. From celebrity panels to cosplay competitions, there's something for every fan of comics, movies, and TV shows.

Chapter 7: Culinary Delights

Dining with a View

Niagara Falls isn't just a feast for the eyes—it's a treat for the taste buds too. we explore the enchanting world of dining with a view, where the mesmerizing scenery becomes the backdrop for a culinary experience like no other.

The Edge Steak & Bar

Situated on the Canadian side, The Edge Steak & Bar offers a dining experience that perfectly complements the breathtaking views of the falls. As you savor a perfectly cooked steak, you'll be treated to a panoramic spectacle of the illuminated falls, creating an ambiance that is both romantic and awe-inspiring. The menu features a fusion of local flavors and international cuisine, ensuring that every dish is a celebration of culinary expertise.

Skylon Tower Revolving Dining Room

Perched atop the iconic Skylon Tower, the Revolving Dining Room takes "dining with a view" to new heights—literally. As you enjoy a gourmet meal, the entire dining room slowly rotates, offering 360-degree views of the falls, the cityscape, and beyond. Whether you're there for lunch or dinner, the changing scenery provides an ever-evolving backdrop for your culinary journey. The menu showcases a diverse selection, from seafood delights to delectable desserts.

Windows by Jamie Kennedy Fresh Grill & Wine Bar

Windows by Jamie Kennedy, located in the Sheraton on the Falls Hotel, combines the culinary artistry of renowned chef Jamie Kennedy with the natural masterpiece of Niagara

Falls. The restaurant's floor-to-ceiling windows frame the falls beautifully, creating a picturesque setting for farm-to-table dishes. The emphasis here is on fresh, locally sourced ingredients that highlight the region's bountiful produce, creating a menu that is as sustainable as it is delicious.

Queen Victoria Place Restaurant

For a dining experience that blends history with a stunning view, Queen Victoria Place Restaurant, nestled in Queen Victoria Park, is a must-visit. Overlooking the American Falls and Bridal Veil Falls, this restaurant offers a casual yet elegant atmosphere. The menu features a variety of dishes crafted with a focus on seasonal ingredients. Whether you're enjoying a leisurely brunch or a romantic dinner, the proximity to the falls adds a touch of natural splendor to every bite.

Watermark Restaurant

Situated in the heart of Niagara Falls' vibrant tourist district, Watermark Restaurant at the Hilton Hotel provides a sophisticated dining experience with unparalleled views of the falls. The menu showcases a blend of contemporary and classic dishes, prepared with precision and creativity. The stylish and modern interior, combined with the ever-present backdrop of cascading water, creates an atmosphere that is both chic and relaxing.

The Keg Steakhouse + Bar

The Keg Steakhouse + Bar, located on the ninth floor of the Embassy Suites Hotel, offers a dining experience that combines the sizzle of perfectly grilled steaks with the spectacle of Niagara Falls. Floor-to-ceiling windows allow diners to enjoy unobstructed views of both the American and

Horseshoe Falls. The menu features a variety of premium steaks and seafood options, ensuring that every visit is a savory delight.

Elements on the Falls

Perched at the brink of the Canadian Horseshoe Falls, Elements on the Falls provides a dining experience that is as close to the falls as it gets. Floor-to-ceiling windows offer uninterrupted views of the thundering waters, creating a dramatic backdrop for your culinary adventure. The menu showcases a fusion of locally inspired dishes and international cuisine, with an emphasis on fresh and seasonal ingredients.

Dining with a view near Niagara Falls is more than a meal—it's a sensory journey that combines the best of culinary artistry with the natural wonders of the falls. Each restaurant on this list offers a unique perspective, ensuring that your dining experience is as memorable as the falls themselves. So, whether you're a food enthusiast, a nature lover, or someone seeking a romantic evening, Niagara Falls has the perfect table reserved for you.

Local Flavors to Try

Niagara Falls isn't just a feast for the eyes; it's a paradise for your taste buds. The region boasts a vibrant culinary scene that reflects the diversity and richness of its surroundings. From farm-fresh produce to exquisite wines, here are some local flavors you must indulge in:

Wines of the Niagara Peninsula:

The Niagara Peninsula is renowned for its vineyards and wineries, producing some of the finest wines in the world. Take a wine tour and savor the flavors of locally produced ice wines, a specialty of the region. The unique climate and fertile soil contribute to the production of these sweet and aromatic wines, making them a must-try for any visitor.

Peaches from Niagara-on-the-Lake:

Niagara-on-the-Lake is celebrated for its succulent peaches, harvested from local orchards. These juicy, sun-ripened peaches are a true taste of summer. Whether you enjoy them fresh or in the form of peach-infused jams and desserts, you're in for a treat. Don't miss the chance to visit a local farmer's market for the freshest picks.

Bison Burgers:

For a unique and hearty culinary experience, try a bison burger. Niagara is home to several farms that raise bison, and many local restaurants incorporate this lean and flavorful meat into their menus. The result is a burger that's not only delicious but also showcases the region's commitment to sustainable and ethical farming practices.

Lake Erie Perch:

Head to the shores of Lake Erie for a taste of the freshest perch. Whether battered and fried to perfection or grilled with local herbs, Lake Erie perch offers a delightful combination of flakiness and flavor. Pair it with a side of hand-cut fries for a classic, mouthwatering meal.

Maple Syrup Delights:

Venture into the nearby maple groves for a sweet experience. Niagara's maple syrup is a true delight, and you can find it drizzled over pancakes at local breakfast spots or infused into specialty candies. During the sugaring-off season, you

may even get the chance to witness the maple syrup production process firsthand.
Apple Varieties:

With numerous orchards dotting the landscape, Niagara is a haven for apple enthusiasts. Depending on the season, you can savor a variety of apples, from crisp and tart to sweet and juicy. Visit an orchard for apple picking or indulge in freshly baked apple pies and ciders at local bakeries.

Artisanal Cheeses:

The dairy farms in the region produce exceptional cheeses that cater to every palate. From creamy brie to sharp cheddars, you'll find a wide array of artisanal cheeses that pair perfectly with local wines. Consider visiting a cheese shop for a curated tasting experience.

Sweet Treats

Niagara Falls isn't just a feast for the eyes; it's also a haven for those with a sweet tooth. The region boasts an array of delightful treats that will satisfy even the most discerning dessert enthusiasts. From iconic classics to innovative creations, here's a tempting journey through the delectable world of Niagara's sweet offerings.
7.3 Sweet Treats

Indulging in sweet treats is a must when visiting Niagara Falls, and the options are as diverse as the falls are powerful. Let your taste buds dance with the variety of confections available.

Maple Syrup Delights: Begin your sweet adventure with a taste of Canada's liquid gold—maple syrup. Local artisans infuse this golden elixir into a range of treats, from maple candies to fluffy maple-infused pancakes. Head to the quaint maple farms dotted around the region to experience the making of this sweet nectar.

Fruit-Filled Pastries: Niagara is renowned for its bountiful orchards, and the local pastry chefs take full advantage of the fresh produce. Sink your teeth into flaky apple turnovers, blueberry tarts, and cherry-stuffed delights. These pastries not only capture the essence of the region but also provide a burst of fruity sweetness.

Ice Cream Extravaganza: When it comes to cooling down on a warm day, Niagara has an array of ice cream parlors that will leave you spoiled for choice. Indulge in unique flavors inspired by the surroundings, like Niagara Peach or Horseshoe Hazelnut. Take a leisurely stroll along the falls while savoring your cone, and let the combination of sweet and scenic views elevate your experience.

Chocolate Bliss: Niagara Falls takes chocolate to a whole new level. Visit the artisanal chocolate shops where skilled chocolatiers craft delectable masterpieces. Whether it's velvety truffles, chocolate-dipped strawberries, or intricately designed bars, each piece is a work of art. Don't forget to explore the cocoa-themed museums to learn about the fascinating journey from bean to bar.

Beavertails by the Falls: A trip to Niagara is incomplete without indulging in the iconic Canadian pastry known as Beavertails. These hand-stretched, whole wheat pastries are deep-fried to golden perfection and can be customized with an array of toppings. Enjoy one with a view of the falls for a truly Canadian experience.

Wine-Infused Desserts: Niagara is celebrated for its vineyards, and the local chefs have ingeniously incorporated wine into their dessert creations. Savor wine-infused cupcakes, sorbets, and even gelato. The marriage of rich, flavorful wines with sweet treats adds a sophisticated touch to your dessert experience.

Butter Tart Trail: Embark on a delicious journey along the Butter Tart Trail, a dedicated route that showcases one of Canada's most beloved desserts—the butter tart. Each bakery along the trail puts its unique spin on this classic treat. The gooey, buttery filling encased in a flaky crust is sure to make your taste buds sing.

In Niagara Falls, every sweet treat tells a story, a tale of the region's rich agricultural heritage and culinary innovation. So, whether you're sipping on a maple latte, savoring a wine-infused cupcake, or biting into a classic butter tart, you're not just enjoying a dessert—you're tasting the essence of Niagara. Indulge, explore, and let the sweetness of the falls linger on your palate as a delicious memory of your visit.

Chapter 8: Family-Friendly Fun

Adventure Parks

Adventure parks near Niagara Falls offer a thrilling escape for visitors of all ages, combining the beauty of nature with adrenaline-pumping activities. From treetop adventures to high-flying ziplines, these parks provide a perfect blend of excitement and natural splendor.

Tree-Top Adventures:
One of the highlights of adventure parks in the region is the exhilarating tree-top adventures. Imagine navigating through a series of suspended bridges, ziplining from one platform to another, and conquering challenging obstacles—all while being surrounded by the lush canopy of trees. These parks often feature courses of varying difficulty levels, ensuring that both beginners and seasoned thrill-seekers can find an appropriate challenge.

Ziplining Across the Gorge:
For those seeking an adrenaline rush with a breathtaking view, ziplining across the gorge is a must-try experience. Soar through the air as you take in the awe-inspiring scenery of Niagara Falls and its surrounding landscapes. Some parks offer nighttime ziplining, providing a unique perspective of the falls illuminated under the night sky—an experience that combines adventure with mesmerizing visuals.

Family-Friendly Adventures:
Adventure parks in the area are designed to cater to families, making them an ideal destination for a day of fun and bonding. From mini-golf courses to gentle ziplines suitable for kids, these parks ensure that everyone in the family can

participate in the excitement. Many parks also incorporate educational elements, teaching visitors about the local flora and fauna, turning the adventure into a learning experience.

Safety First:
Safety is a top priority at these adventure parks. Before embarking on any activity, visitors are provided with comprehensive safety briefings and are equipped with state-of-the-art harnesses and gear. Trained guides accompany participants through the courses, ensuring that everyone can enjoy the thrills with confidence.

Combo Packages:
To maximize the adventure experience, many parks offer combo packages that include access to multiple activities. This means visitors can seamlessly transition from ziplining to tree-top adventures and perhaps end the day with a scenic hike. Combo packages often provide a cost-effective way to enjoy a variety of activities, making the most out of your visit.

Photographic Opportunities:
Adventure parks near Niagara Falls provide not only a rush of excitement but also incredible photographic opportunities. Capture candid moments of family members conquering challenges, or take in the panoramic views from the highest points of the courses. The parks are designed not only for adventure enthusiasts but also for those seeking to document their memorable experiences in a stunning natural setting.

Butterfly Conservatory

Nestled near the majestic Niagara Falls, the Butterfly Conservatory is a enchanting haven that captivates visitors with its kaleidoscope of colors and delicate fluttering wings. Located within the lush grounds of the Niagara Parks

Botanical Gardens, this chapter will explore the wonders that await within the walls of the Butterfly Conservatory.

The Butterfly Conservatory is a haven for nature lovers and those seeking a serene escape from the bustling energy of the falls. As you enter, you are immediately transported into a tropical paradise. The air is warm and humid, mimicking the natural habitat of these delicate creatures. Lush greenery surrounds you, creating a perfect environment for a thriving butterfly population.

The conservatory boasts a stunning collection of over 2,000 vibrantly colored butterflies, representing numerous species from around the world. Walking through the conservatory feels like stepping into a living, breathing work of art. Butterflies of all shapes and sizes gracefully dance through the air, their wings adorned with intricate patterns and hues that range from vibrant oranges and blues to subtle earthy tones.

One of the highlights of the Butterfly Conservatory is the opportunity for up-close encounters with these winged wonders. Butterflies may land gently on your shoulder or hand, allowing for a magical and immersive experience. Visitors often find themselves surrounded by a fluttering kaleidoscope, creating a sense of connection with the natural world.

The conservatory is not only a visual feast but also an educational experience. Knowledgeable guides are on hand to provide insights into the life cycle of butterflies, their behaviors, and the importance of conservation efforts. It's a chance to learn about the intricate dance between flowers and butterflies, as well as the role these creatures play in maintaining the balance of ecosystems.

For those with a passion for photography, the Butterfly Conservatory offers a myriad of opportunities to capture breathtaking moments. Patiently waiting for a butterfly to alight on a flower or a sunbeam to filter through the tropical foliage can result in stunning and unique shots that showcase the beauty of nature.

To enhance the experience, the conservatory often hosts special events and exhibitions. These may include themed butterfly releases, where newly emerged butterflies take their first flight in the conservatory, creating a magical spectacle. The events provide an extra layer of enchantment and are perfect for families, nature enthusiasts, and anyone looking to immerse themselves in the world of butterflies.

Before leaving, visitors can explore the gift shop, which offers a variety of butterfly-themed souvenirs, educational materials, and locally crafted items. It's a chance to take home a piece of the magic and continue supporting the conservation efforts of the Butterfly Conservatory.

Educational Excursions

Niagara Falls isn't just a breathtaking natural wonder; it's also a fantastic destination for educational adventures that stimulate both the mind and the senses. we'll delve into the enriching world of educational excursions around the Niagara Falls area.

1. Discovering Marine Life: Aquarium of Niagara

One educational gem near the falls is the Aquarium of Niagara. This facility offers an immersive experience into the underwater world of the Great Lakes and beyond. Visitors can explore interactive exhibits showcasing marine life, learn about conservation efforts, and even participate in educational programs. From seahorses to sharks, the aquarium provides a fascinating look into the diverse ecosystems connected to Niagara Falls.

2. Geological Wonders: Niagara Gorge Discovery Center

For those fascinated by the geological forces that shaped Niagara Falls, the Niagara Gorge Discovery Center is a must-visit. This center offers insightful exhibits detailing the formation of the falls, the ancient history of the region, and the unique flora and fauna found in the Niagara Gorge. Educational programs and guided hikes provide in-depth knowledge about the geological wonders surrounding the falls.

3. History Lessons: Old Fort Niagara

Step back in time with a visit to Old Fort Niagara, a historic site that has witnessed centuries of events. This well-preserved fort allows visitors to explore military architecture, artifacts, and reenactments from the colonial era. Educational tours cover topics ranging from military strategy to the cultural exchanges that occurred in this strategic location.

4. The Power of Hydroelectricity: Niagara Power Vista

Delve into the world of energy and hydroelectric power at the Niagara Power Vista. This interactive visitor center provides a captivating journey through the history of harnessing the immense power of the falls for electricity. Educational exhibits explain the science behind hydroelectricity, offering an engaging experience for students and curious minds alike.

5. Environmental Education: Niagara Parks Butterfly Conservatory

While known for its stunning array of butterflies, the Butterfly Conservatory is also a hub for environmental education. Visitors can learn about the life cycle of butterflies, the importance of pollinators, and the delicate balance of ecosystems. The conservatory often hosts educational programs and workshops, making it an ideal destination for nature enthusiasts and students.

6. Indigenous Perspectives: Niagara Parks Heritage Trail

Embark on a journey along the Niagara Parks Heritage Trail, where the rich indigenous history of the region comes to life. Educational markers and guided tours provide insights into the cultural significance of the falls for the First Nations people. This excursion offers a valuable opportunity to learn about the traditions, stories, and enduring connection of indigenous communities to Niagara Falls.

Chapter 9: Nightlife by the Falls

Waterfront Bars

As the sun sets over the majestic Niagara Falls, the vibrant nightlife comes to life, and one of the best ways to experience it is by visiting the enchanting waterfront bars that line the shores. These establishments not only offer a respite from the day's adventures but also provide an unparalleled view of the illuminated falls, creating a magical atmosphere for an unforgettable night out.

The Fallsview Lounge

Nestled on the Canadian side, The Fallsview Lounge stands as a testament to sophistication and panoramic views. Perched high above the falls, this waterfront gem offers an extensive selection of cocktails and local wines. The floor-to-ceiling windows allow patrons to revel in the mesmerizing sight of the falls lit up in a kaleidoscope of colors. As you sip on your drink, the distant roar of the falls serves as a melodic backdrop, creating an ambiance that perfectly complements the natural wonder just outside.

Rapids Bar & Grill

Situated on the American side, Rapids Bar & Grill provides a more casual yet equally captivating experience. The outdoor patio overlooks the turbulent rapids leading to the falls, offering a front-row seat to the raw power of the Niagara River. The bar menu boasts a variety of craft beers and signature cocktails, making it an ideal spot to unwind after a day of exploration. With the falls in the background and the gentle rustle of the river, Rapids Bar & Grill captures the essence of Niagara's natural beauty.

Misty Pints

For those seeking a more immersive experience, Misty Pints, located at the base of the falls, provides an up-close encounter with the misty ambiance created by the powerful cascades. This open-air bar offers a refreshing selection of locally brewed beers and inventive cocktails. The atmosphere is lively, with the falls providing a breathtaking backdrop as you enjoy your drink. Misty Pints is a favorite among those looking to feel the energy of the falls in a more intimate setting.

Niagara's waterfront bars not only cater to the drink enthusiast but also elevate the overall nightlife experience with live music, themed nights, and friendly locals. Whether you're sipping a classic cocktail while gazing at the illuminated falls or enjoying a cold beer with the sounds of the rapids in the background, these bars offer a diverse range of experiences that capture the essence of Niagara's enchanting evenings.

As the night progresses and the falls transform into a shimmering curtain of light, the waterfront bars become a hub of social activity, making them an essential part of any visitor's itinerary. Whether you prefer a quiet evening with a view or a lively night filled with laughter and music, the waterfront bars near Niagara Falls offer a unique and unforgettable nightlife experience that perfectly complements the natural beauty of this iconic destination.

Nighttime Illumination

As the sun sets and darkness descends over Niagara Falls, a magical transformation takes place. The already awe-inspiring natural wonder becomes a canvas for a dazzling display of lights, enchanting visitors in a spectacle known as Nighttime Illumination.

Illuminating the Falls:

The illumination of Niagara Falls is a tradition that dates back to the late 19th century, and it has evolved into a sophisticated and mesmerizing display in the modern era. Powerful lights strategically positioned on the Canadian side of the falls project a spectrum of colors onto the rushing waters, creating a visual symphony that dances with the mist rising from the cascading falls.

The Technicolor Dream:

Nighttime Illumination is not a static affair; it's an ever-changing palette that bathes the falls in a rainbow of colors. The vibrant hues reflect off the mist, creating a dynamic and ethereal experience. The Falls are often bathed in shades of blue, green, red, and purple, creating an atmosphere that is both romantic and mysterious.

Special Illumination Events:

Beyond the regular nightly display, there are special events that elevate the illumination experience. Seasonal themes, holidays, and even awareness campaigns are celebrated through unique lighting arrangements. Imagine the falls bathed in red and white for Canada Day or adorned in pink for breast cancer awareness—it's a breathtaking sight that adds an extra layer of significance to the natural wonder.

Viewing Points:

Several vantage points offer optimal views of the illuminated Niagara Falls. The Queen Victoria Park and Table Rock Welcome Centre on the Canadian side provide unobstructed views, allowing visitors to witness the falls in all their illuminated glory. The American side also offers spectacular viewpoints, with Niagara State Park providing a quieter, contemplative setting.

Illumination Cruises:

For a truly immersive experience, consider taking an illumination cruise. These boat tours take you close to the falls just as the lights begin to cast their spell. The play of lights on the mist, combined with the sound of the roaring falls, creates a sensory experience that's nothing short of magical.

Photography Under the Lights:

Nighttime Illumination is a photographer's dream. The interplay of light and water presents unique challenges and opportunities for capturing stunning shots. Long exposure shots bring out the ethereal quality of the falls, and the ever-changing colors provide photographers with an endless array of creative possibilities.

Practical Tips for Visitors:

If you're planning to witness the Nighttime Illumination at Niagara Falls, consider these practical tips. Check the illumination schedule in advance, as it may vary seasonally. Dress warmly, especially during cooler months, and bring a camera to capture the breathtaking scenes. If you're on the Canadian side, explore nearby observation points for different perspectives.

Stargazing Over the Falls

In the quiet embrace of the night, Niagara Falls transforms into a celestial wonder, offering a breathtaking canvas for stargazing enthusiasts. As the day's tumultuous waters settle, a serene atmosphere descends upon the falls, revealing a different kind of beauty—one that extends far beyond the rushing waters and mist. In Chapter 9.3, we embark on a cosmic journey, exploring the magic of stargazing over the falls.

The Perfect Night Sky

The Niagara night sky, unmarred by the glow of city lights, becomes a celestial masterpiece. Underneath the vast expanse of stars, the falls take on an ethereal glow, creating a surreal juxtaposition between the earthly wonders and the cosmic ballet above. Stargazers are treated to a symphony of constellations, planets, and, if lucky, meteor showers that add an extra dash of magic to the experience.

Ideal Stargazing Spots

Discovering the ideal spot to lay out a blanket and tilt your head upward is an adventure in itself. Niagara Parks, with its commitment to preserving the natural beauty of the area, provides designated stargazing areas near the falls. Away from the hustle and bustle, these locations offer an unobstructed view of the night sky, allowing visitors to immerse themselves in the celestial wonders.

Guided Stargazing Tours

For those seeking a more immersive experience, guided stargazing tours are available. Knowledgeable astronomers lead groups to prime stargazing locations, offering insights into the constellations, planets, and astronomical phenomena that grace the Niagara night sky. Telescopes enhance the view, bringing distant stars and planets within reach, creating a captivating learning experience for visitors of all ages.

9.3.4 Celestial Events Calendar

Timing is crucial when it comes to stargazing, and Niagara Falls boasts a celestial events calendar that rivals any astronomical enthusiast's dream. From meteor showers to planetary alignments, the falls play host to a variety of celestial events throughout the year. Chapter 9.3.4 provides a comprehensive guide, ensuring that visitors can plan their trips to coincide with these awe-inspiring occurrences.

Stargazing Photography Tips

Capturing the brilliance of the night sky over Niagara Falls requires a unique set of photography skills. Chapter 9.3.5 delves into the art of astrophotography, offering tips on capturing the perfect shot of the falls against a backdrop of stars. From long exposure techniques to recommended camera gear, aspiring night photographers will find valuable insights to elevate their craft.

The Spiritual Connection

Beyond the scientific allure of stargazing, there's a spiritual connection that many feel when immersed in the tranquility of the night. The sound of the falls becomes a cosmic lullaby, and the starlit sky serves as a reminder of our place in the universe. Visitors often describe this experience as a moment of introspection, a chance to connect with the sublime forces that shape both the heavens and the earth.

Chapter 10: Hidden Gems

Off the Beaten Path

While Niagara Falls is undeniably captivating, there's a world beyond the well-trodden tourist spots waiting to be discovered. we embark on a journey to explore the hidden gems and offbeat wonders that often escape the casual traveler's radar.

1. The Enchanting Glen Nature Reserve

Tucked away from the bustling crowds, the Glen Nature Reserve offers a serene escape into untouched wilderness. Venture along meandering trails that lead to hidden waterfalls and panoramic viewpoints. The air is filled with the sweet scent of wildflowers, and the only sounds are the rustling leaves and distant bird calls. It's a nature lover's haven.

2. Riverside Artisan Villages

A short drive from the falls unveils charming artisan villages along the riverbanks. Here, local craftsmen and artists showcase their talents in quaint studios. Stroll through cobblestone streets lined with handcrafted goods, from unique jewelry to bespoke pottery. Engage with the artisans, and you might find yourself taking home a piece of Niagara's local artistry.

3. The Forgotten Caves Expedition

For the adventurous souls, consider the Forgotten Caves Expedition. Away from the conventional tourist routes, these caves tell tales of centuries past. Guided tours lead you through winding underground passages adorned with stalactites and stalagmites. It's an immersive journey into the geological history of the region, providing a stark contrast to the thunderous beauty of the falls.

4. Sunrise at DeVeaux Woods State Park

Escape the sunrise crowds at the popular viewpoints and head to DeVeaux Woods State Park for a more intimate experience. As the sun paints the sky with hues of pink and orange, the quietude of the park amplifies the magic of the moment. Take a leisurely stroll along wooded trails, and you might encounter local wildlife awakening to the new day.

5. Hidden Culinary Gems

Beyond the well-known eateries, offbeat culinary gems await discovery. Venture into neighborhood bistros and family-owned establishments serving dishes that tell a story of local flavors. From artisanal cheese shops to quaint cafes with a view, these hidden culinary spots promise a delightful gastronomic adventure.

Secret Scenic Spots

Discovering hidden gems around Niagara Falls goes beyond the popular tourist attractions. In this chapter, we unveil the mystery behind some secret scenic spots that promise solitude, breathtaking views, and a deeper connection with nature.

1. Luna's Cove:
Tucked away from the bustling crowds, Luna's Cove is a secluded spot offering a mesmerizing view of the falls. Accessible through a serene hiking trail, the cove provides a unique vantage point, allowing visitors to witness the falls in all their glory without the typical throngs of tourists.

2. Whispering Pines Outlook:
For those seeking a peaceful retreat, the Whispering Pines Outlook is a hidden haven. The elevated vantage point provides a panoramic view of the entire Niagara region, surrounded by the soothing rustle of pine trees. It's an ideal spot for quiet contemplation and connecting with the natural beauty of the area.

3. Serenity Garden Bridge:
This charming bridge is nestled within a secret garden, offering a picturesque view of the falls. The bridge is adorned with vibrant flowers and offers a unique perspective, making it a perfect spot for photographers looking to capture the falls in a more intimate setting.

4. Crystal Cavern Overlook:
Venture off the beaten path to discover the Crystal Cavern Overlook, a hidden gem that combines the beauty of natural rock formations with a stunning view of the falls. The cavern creates a frame around the cascading waters, creating a magical and surreal experience for those lucky enough to find it.

5. Aurora Point:
Named for the spectacular Northern Lights displays occasionally visible from this location, Aurora Point offers a peaceful setting to admire the falls. Surrounded by lush greenery, it's an ideal spot for a quiet picnic or a romantic evening watching the lights dance over the water.

6. Solitude Shoreline:
Escape the crowds and find solace along the Solitude Shoreline. This secluded stretch of the riverbank provides an unobstructed view of the falls, allowing visitors to immerse themselves in the natural symphony of rushing water and chirping birds without the distractions of large crowds.

7. Enchanted Outlook:
True to its name, the Enchanted Outlook is a hidden viewpoint that seems almost otherworldly. Accessed through a winding forest trail, the outlook unveils a spellbinding panorama of the falls framed by the lush foliage, creating a sense of enchantment and wonder.

8. Harmony Hill Overpass:
For a unique perspective, venture to the Harmony Hill Overpass. This elevated location provides a bird's-eye view of the falls and the surrounding landscape. It's a particularly magical spot during sunrise and sunset when the sky is painted in hues of pink and orange.

9. Tranquil Tunnels:
Explore the Tranquil Tunnels, a network of hidden pathways that lead to secluded spots along the river. These tunnels, carved by nature over the years, offer a sense of adventure as you discover quiet corners where you can appreciate the falls away from the more frequented areas.

10. Rainbow's End Retreat:
Nestled at the end of a secret trail, Rainbow's End Retreat is a serene escape offering a close-up view of the rainbows formed by the mist of the falls. It's a tranquil spot to reflect on the natural wonders and find inspiration in the ever-changing colors of the landscape.

These secret scenic spots invite the intrepid traveler to go beyond the obvious and embrace the hidden beauty that Niagara Falls has to offer. Whether you seek solitude, romance, or simply a unique perspective, these spots promise an unforgettable experience away from the crowds.

Local Favorites

Niagara Falls is not just a destination; it's a community with its own unique charm and flavor. As you explore the area, be sure to immerse yourself in the local favorites that capture the essence of life around the falls.

1. Mom-and-Pop Cafés:

One of the true delights of Niagara Falls is its collection of charming mom-and-pop cafés. These cozy establishments not only serve exceptional coffee but also provide a welcoming atmosphere that feels like home. Locals often gather here to share stories, and you'll likely find some of the best homemade pastries and treats.

2. Artisanal Shops:

Nestled amidst the more commercialized areas, you'll discover hidden gems—artisanal shops run by local craftsmen and artists. These shops showcase handmade jewelry, unique artworks, and crafts that reflect the creativity of the Niagara community. It's an excellent opportunity to take home a one-of-a-kind souvenir.

3. Farmers' Markets:

Experience the vibrant local agriculture scene by visiting one of Niagara Falls' farmers' markets. Here, you can sample fresh produce, artisan cheeses, and homemade preserves. Engage with local farmers and vendors, and perhaps, enjoy a picnic with your market finds in one of the scenic parks nearby.

4. Community Events:

The heart of any community lies in its events, and Niagara Falls is no exception. Check out the local event calendar for festivals, parades, and gatherings that bring the community together. Whether it's a music festival or a celebration of local heritage, participating in these events offers a unique window into the spirit of Niagara.

5. Historical Landmarks:

Delve into the history of Niagara Falls by exploring its lesser-known historical landmarks. Local favorites often include old churches, heritage homes, and buildings that hold tales of times gone by. Consider taking a guided walking tour to uncover the fascinating stories behind these structures.

6. Neighborhood Pubs:

For a taste of authentic local life, step into one of the neighborhood pubs. These establishments are not just about the drinks; they are communal spaces where locals gather after work or on weekends. Engage in conversations, try regional brews, and savor hearty pub fare.

7. Community Gardens:

Experience the beauty of community collaboration in Niagara's community gardens. These green spaces not only contribute to the city's aesthetics but also foster a sense of togetherness. Join a guided tour to learn about the local flora and the efforts put into maintaining these serene gardens.

8. Live Music Venues:

Niagara Falls has a thriving local music scene, and there's no better way to experience it than by visiting a live music venue. Check out local bands, solo artists, or even open mic nights. It's an opportunity to enjoy diverse musical talents and support the local arts.

9. Recreational Parks:

Beyond the tourist attractions, locals have their favorite parks for leisure and recreation. These parks often have jogging trails, picnic spots, and serene corners that offer a break from the hustle and bustle. Join in on a game of frisbee, or simply unwind with a book under the shade of a tree.

10. Family-Run Bed and Breakfasts:

While the falls attract numerous visitors, locals often prefer the cozy ambiance of family-run bed and breakfasts. These establishments not only provide comfortable lodging but also offer a more personalized experience, with hosts who can share insider tips on the best local spots.

In embracing these local favorites, you'll not only witness the natural beauty of Niagara Falls but also immerse yourself in the warmth and character of the community that calls this place home. So, go ahead, wander off the beaten path, and discover the heart of Niagara.

Chapter 11: Day Trips and Beyond

Exploring Nearby Towns

Beyond the thundering beauty of Niagara Falls lie charming towns that offer a unique blend of history, culture, and local flair. Exploring these nearby gems not only provides a welcome respite from the bustling energy of the falls but also unveils hidden treasures waiting to be discovered.

1. Historic Niagara-on-the-Lake

Venture down the scenic Niagara Parkway, and you'll find yourself in the quaint town of Niagara-on-the-Lake. Steeped in history, this charming town boasts cobblestone streets, heritage buildings, and a timeless ambiance. Explore boutique shops offering artisanal crafts, indulge in culinary delights at cozy cafes, and take a leisurely stroll through the lush gardens of the renowned Niagara Parks School of Horticulture.

2. Charming Lewiston, USA

Crossing the border into the United States, Lewiston welcomes you with its small-town charm and rich history. Nestled along the banks of the Niagara River, this picturesque town offers a blend of art galleries, antique shops, and a vibrant local arts scene. Don't miss the Lewiston Art Festival if you happen to visit in the summer, showcasing the creativity of local and international artists.

3. Port Dalhousie: A Lakeside Retreat

Just a short drive north of the falls, Port Dalhousie beckons with its lakeside charm. Explore the historic Lakeside Park Carousel, enjoy a leisurely stroll along the pier, and savor the tranquility of Lake Ontario. For a unique experience, try the Lakeside Beach Club, a local favorite offering breathtaking views of the lake and delicious waterfront dining.

4. Quaint Jordan Village

Nestled in the heart of Niagara's wine country, Jordan Village is a must-visit for wine enthusiasts and those seeking a serene escape. Explore boutique wineries, sample exquisite vintages, and indulge in farm-to-table dining experiences. The Jordan Village Antiques and Art District offers a delightful shopping experience, with unique finds that reflect the essence of the region.

5. Picturesque Beamsville

Known for its scenic vineyards and orchards, Beamsville invites you to explore the beauty of the Niagara Escarpment. Take a wine tour through the Beamsville Bench wineries, offering award-winning wines and panoramic views. The Bruce Trail, running along the escarpment, provides hiking enthusiasts with a chance to immerse themselves in nature and capture stunning vistas of the surrounding landscape.

Exploring nearby towns adds a delightful layer to your Niagara Falls adventure. Each town has its own character, offering a glimpse into the region's diverse tapestry. Whether you're drawn to the historic charm of Niagara-on-the-Lake, the artistic vibes of Lewiston, the lakeside tranquility of Port Dalhousie, the wine country allure of Jordan Village, or the natural beauty of Beamsville, these nearby gems promise to enrich your Niagara experience with memories that extend beyond the falls themselves. So, set forth on a journey of discovery and let the neighboring towns weave their own stories into your Niagara Falls adventure

Winery Tours

Wine enthusiasts and novices alike will find the Niagara region to be a haven for exquisite winery experiences. The lush landscapes, complemented by the misty backdrop of the falls, create a unique terroir that contributes to the production of world-class wines. we'll explore the delightful world of winery tours and why they are an essential part of any visit to Niagara.

Discovering Terroir:

Niagara's wineries boast a rich diversity of grape varietals, thanks to the region's unique climate and soil composition. A winery tour offers more than just a tasting; it's a journey through the terroir, where visitors can witness the meticulous processes involved in winemaking. From vine to bottle, you'll gain insight into the art and science of producing exceptional wines.

Scenic Vineyard Tours:

Embarking on a winery tour in Niagara is not just about the wine; it's about the breathtaking scenery that accompanies the vineyards. Many wineries offer guided tours through their sprawling vineyards, providing an opportunity to stroll among the grapevines, learning about the different varieties and the cultivation process. The panoramic views of the Niagara Escarpment and the falls in the distance add an extra layer of enchantment to the experience.

Tasting Sessions with Experts:

Winery tours culminate in tasting sessions where visitors can savor a selection of wines crafted on-site. Knowledgeable and passionate sommeliers guide participants through the nuances of each wine, from the light and crisp whites to the bold and complex reds. These experts share the stories behind the wines, offering a deeper understanding of the craftsmanship involved.

Food and Wine Pairing:

Many wineries in the Niagara region go beyond the standard wine tastings by offering curated food and wine pairing experiences. Delight your taste buds as you discover the perfect marriage of flavors between local cheeses, charcuterie, and the winery's finest selections. This gastronomic adventure enhances the overall sensory pleasure of the tour.

Unique Winery Events:

Throughout the year, Niagara's wineries host a variety of events that elevate the wine-tasting experience. From grape stomping festivals to winemaker dinners, these events provide an opportunity to engage with the winemaking community, learn about new releases, and celebrate the region's vinicultural heritage.

Sustainable Practices:

Environmental consciousness is a growing trend in the wine industry, and Niagara's wineries are no exception. Many wineries in the region have adopted sustainable practices in their vineyards and cellars. A winery tour becomes not only an exploration of flavors but also an insight into the eco-friendly initiatives that contribute to the preservation of the region's natural beauty.

Adventure Across the Border

As you stand by the mesmerizing Niagara Falls, you might be tempted to extend your adventure beyond borders. Crossing into neighboring regions opens up a world of possibilities, adding an international flair to your experience.

1. Exploring Canada: Beyond the Falls

Toronto Excursions

A short drive from Niagara Falls, Toronto beckons with its vibrant city life and iconic landmarks. The CN Tower, standing tall in the skyline, offers panoramic views of the city and the Great Lake Ontario. Explore the diverse neighborhoods, from the historic Distillery District to the trendy Queen Street West, where you can indulge in shopping and diverse culinary delights.

Niagara-on-the-Lake

Known for its charming 19th-century architecture and picturesque vineyards, Niagara-on-the-Lake is a must-visit. Take a leisurely stroll through its quaint streets, indulge in wine tasting at world-class wineries, and catch a play at the renowned Shaw Festival Theatre.

Canadian Culture and Cuisine

Immerse yourself in Canadian culture by visiting museums like the Royal Ontario Museum or the Art Gallery of Ontario. Don't miss the chance to savor Canadian specialties at local eateries, from poutine to butter tarts.

2. Crossing into the United States

Buffalo, New York

Just a short drive from Niagara Falls, Buffalo offers a mix of history, art, and culinary delights. Explore the Buffalo and Erie County Naval & Military Park, showcasing historic naval vessels. The Albright-Knox Art Gallery is a haven for art enthusiasts, housing an impressive collection of modern and contemporary art.

Niagara Falls State Park, USA

While the falls themselves are shared between the United States and Canada, the American side offers a unique perspective. Take the Cave of the Winds tour to get up close and personal with the Bridal Veil Falls, or stroll along the scenic trails of Niagara Falls State Park.

Adventure in Buffalo's Outdoors

For the outdoor enthusiast, Buffalo's parks and waterfront provide ample opportunities for adventure. Kayak along the Buffalo River, hike the trails of Chestnut Ridge Park, or enjoy a relaxing day at Delaware Park.

3. Practical Tips for Cross-Border Adventures

Passport and Documentation

Before embarking on your cross-border adventure, ensure you have a valid passport and any necessary travel documentation. Familiarize yourself with the entry requirements for both Canada and the United States.

Currency Exchange

Be mindful of currency differences. While major establishments in tourist areas may accept both Canadian and U.S. dollars, it's advisable to have local currency on hand for a seamless experience.

Transportation

Explore various transportation options, from guided tours to self-driving. Consider the convenience of border-crossing services to streamline your journey.

Embarking on an adventure across the border adds a dynamic layer to your Niagara Falls experience. Whether you find yourself exploring the vibrant streets of Toronto, savoring the wines of Niagara-on-the-Lake, or discovering the cultural gems of Buffalo, the possibilities are as vast and diverse as the landscapes you encounter. Enjoy the richness of two nations intertwined by the awe-inspiring wonder of Niagara Falls.

Chapter 12: Relaxation and Wellness

Spas with a View

The spas in the region offer a unique blend of relaxation and breathtaking views. This section is dedicated to those seeking a pampering experience amidst the natural beauty of the falls.

Serene Escapes Spa

One standout spa in the area is the Serene Escapes Spa, strategically located to provide patrons with a front-row seat to the majestic Niagara Falls. As you indulge in a rejuvenating massage or a calming facial, large panoramic windows frame the cascading waters, creating a tranquil ambiance that enhances the spa experience.

The spa's design seamlessly integrates with the surrounding environment, using natural elements to complement the exterior beauty. Imagine unwinding with a hot stone massage while gazing at the powerful rush of water just outside your window. The rhythmic sound of the falls becomes part of the spa's soundtrack, enhancing the overall sense of tranquility.

Zen Over the Gorge Spa

Another gem is the Zen Over the Gorge Spa, perched on the cliffs overlooking the Niagara Gorge. This spa takes relaxation to new heights, quite literally. As you enjoy a soak in an outdoor hot tub or receive a soothing body wrap, the panoramic views of the winding river below and the lush greenery create a sense of serenity that is unparalleled.

The spa's architecture is designed to maximize the visual experience. Floor-to-ceiling windows and outdoor terraces provide guests with unobstructed views, allowing them to feel a profound connection with nature. It's not just a spa day; it's a journey into the heart of Niagara's beauty.

Exclusive Rooftop Retreat Spa

For those who seek exclusivity, the Exclusive Rooftop Retreat Spa offers an intimate setting with private treatment rooms and a rooftop lounge. From this vantage point, guests can savor a bird's-eye view of both the American and Canadian falls. The spa's menu is as diverse as its views, offering everything from holistic massages to rejuvenating facials.

The rooftop lounge is a key feature, allowing patrons to extend their relaxation with a post-treatment herbal tea or a glass of local wine. As the sun sets over the falls, the atmosphere transforms into a magical panorama of colors, making it an ideal spot for couples seeking a romantic retreat.

In addition to the spas mentioned, Niagara Falls boasts several other wellness havens that seamlessly blend luxurious treatments with the natural wonders of the region. Each spa, in its unique way, offers a sensory journey that goes beyond the physical touch, immersing guests in the awe-inspiring beauty that surrounds Niagara Falls.

Yoga Retreats

In the bustling atmosphere around Niagara Falls, where the thunderous roar of the falls echoes through the air, finding moments of serenity might seem like a challenge. However, tucked away in the heart of the region, Chapter 12.2 beckons those seeking balance and rejuvenation—Yoga Retreats.

Yoga Retreats: A Haven of Tranquility

Niagara Falls, often synonymous with excitement and adventure, surprises visitors with its offering of yoga retreats that provide a haven of tranquility amid the natural grandeur. These retreats are designed to seamlessly blend the mesmerizing energy of the falls with the ancient practice of yoga, creating an experience that nurtures both body and soul.

1. Connecting with Nature

Imagine striking a warrior pose as the morning sun casts a golden glow over the falls. Yoga retreats in the Niagara region often capitalize on the stunning natural surroundings, offering open-air sessions with panoramic views. Engaging in yoga amidst nature's symphony, with the falls as a backdrop, brings a unique sense of grounding and connection.

2. Varied Practices for All Levels

Whether you're a seasoned yogi or a beginner, these retreats cater to all levels of expertise. Experienced instructors guide participants through a variety of practices, from gentle Hatha yoga to more dynamic Vinyasa flows. The goal is not just physical wellness but also to encourage mental clarity and emotional balance.

3. Mindful Meditation

In addition to yoga sessions, retreats in the Niagara Falls region often include mindfulness meditation. Picture yourself sitting in stillness, the sound of waterfalls serving as a natural meditation soundtrack. The combination of meditation and the powerful energy of the falls creates a unique environment for introspection and self-discovery.

4. Wellness Beyond Yoga

Yoga retreats here extend beyond the mat. Many offer holistic wellness experiences, including spa treatments, nature walks, and nutritional workshops. It's a comprehensive approach to well-being that ensures visitors leave not only relaxed but also armed with tools for a healthier lifestyle.

5. Community and Connection

Participating in a yoga retreat is not just a solo journey; it's an opportunity to connect with like-minded individuals. Whether you're traveling alone or with friends, the communal aspect of these retreats fosters a sense of unity. Sharing the practice with others, perhaps under the guidance of a skilled yogi, creates bonds that often extend beyond the retreat itself.

6. Choosing Your Retreat

Niagara Falls offers a range of yoga retreats, each with its unique flavor. Some are weekend getaways, while others may be week-long immersions. From luxury retreats with spa amenities to more rustic experiences that focus on simplicity, there's a diverse array of options to suit individual preferences.

Chapter 13: Adrenaline Adventures

Helicopter Rides

Embarking on a helicopter ride provides an unparalleled perspective of the majestic falls. As the rotor blades begin to spin and the aircraft lifts off, the panoramic view unfolds before passengers, revealing the awe-inspiring beauty of the cascading waters. The thunderous roar of the falls, usually heard from ground level, transforms into a distant melody as the helicopter ascends.

The Route of Wonders

Helicopter tours typically follow a carefully planned route that showcases not only the falls but also the surrounding landscapes. Passengers can expect to witness the verdant greenery of Niagara Parks, the winding Niagara River, and the iconic Horseshoe Falls from a vantage point that few get to experience. The rainbow-hued mist rising from the falls creates a surreal atmosphere, adding to the enchantment of the journey.

Thrills and Chills

For those seeking an adrenaline rush, helicopter rides above Niagara Falls offer an exhilarating experience. Skilled pilots navigate the helicopter with precision, performing gentle turns and smooth maneuvers to ensure passengers get the best possible views without compromising safety. The combination of breathtaking scenery and the thrill of flight makes this adventure an unforgettable one.

Day and Night Magic

Helicopter rides are not limited to daylight hours; some operators offer tours that extend into the evening, allowing passengers to witness the falls illuminated by the vibrant colors of nighttime lights. The cascading water takes on a different persona after sunset, creating a magical ambiance that adds a new dimension to the experience. The city lights, the moon's glow, and the falls' illumination create a canvas of visual delights.

Choosing the Right Tour

With several helicopter tour operators in the region, visitors have the flexibility to choose a ride that suits their preferences. Some tours focus solely on the falls, providing an extended and comprehensive exploration, while others may include additional landmarks and attractions in the itinerary. The duration of the ride, the type of helicopter used, and any add-on experiences should be considered when selecting a tour.

Making Memories

Helicopter rides over Niagara Falls are not just about the sights but also about the memories created during the journey. Whether it's a solo adventure, a romantic escapade for couples, or a thrilling family outing, the shared experience of seeing one of the world's natural wonders from the sky forms lasting impressions.

White-Water Rafting

White-water rafting near Niagara Falls is an exhilarating adventure that promises an adrenaline rush amid the natural beauty of the region. The roaring rapids of the Niagara River provide an ideal setting for this thrilling water sport, attracting adventure enthusiasts from all around the world.

The Rapids:

The stretch of the Niagara River for white-water rafting is particularly known for its challenging rapids, offering an exciting and dynamic experience for both beginners and seasoned rafters. The rapids are categorized based on their difficulty levels, ranging from Class I to Class VI, with Class VI being the most challenging. The diversity of the rapids ensures that there's an option suitable for everyone, from families looking for a fun day out to adrenaline junkies seeking an intense rush.

Planning Your Rafting Trip:

Before embarking on a white-water rafting adventure, it's crucial to plan accordingly. Many reputable outfitters in the area provide guided tours, ensuring safety while delivering an unforgettable experience. These tours typically include expert guides who are well-versed in navigating the rapids, along with providing essential safety instructions and equipment.

Choosing the Right Rapids:

For beginners, opting for Class I to III rapids is recommended, as these offer a good balance of excitement without being overly challenging. Those seeking a more intense experience can venture into the higher classes. Popular rapids for white-water rafting near Niagara Falls include the Devil's Hole Rapids, Whirlpool Rapids, and the thrilling Class V Ellicottville Rapids.

The Thrill of the Adventure:

Once on the water, the sheer power and unpredictability of the rapids become apparent. Paddling through the frothy waves, feeling the cold mist from the rushing water, and working as a team to navigate through the twists and turns of the river create a sense of camaraderie among rafters. It's not just about conquering the rapids but also about enjoying the breathtaking scenery that surrounds the Niagara River.

Safety First:

Safety is paramount in white-water rafting, and outfitters take extensive measures to ensure a secure experience. Rafters are provided with proper safety gear, including life jackets and helmets. Guides are trained to handle emergency situations and to navigate through challenging spots in the river. Following safety guidelines and listening to the instructions of the guide are crucial for a successful and secure white-water rafting experience.

Unwinding After the Adventure:

After the thrilling descent down the rapids, many rafting tours offer a chance to unwind and share stories. Some outfitters provide post-rafting amenities like hot showers, changing rooms, and even a riverside picnic, allowing participants to relax and relive the excitement of the adventure.

Ziplining Across the Gorge

Embarking on the adventure of ziplining across the gorge near Niagara Falls is an exhilarating experience that promises a unique perspective of the breathtaking natural wonder. Here, we delve into the details of this adrenaline-pumping activity, providing readers with insights into what to expect and how to make the most of this thrilling escapade.

The Launch Point

As you gear up for your ziplining adventure, you'll find yourself at a carefully chosen launch point, strategically positioned to offer panoramic views of the gorge and the cascading falls. The anticipation builds as you step into your harness, secured by expert guides who prioritize safety while ensuring an unforgettable experience.

The Adrenaline Rush

Once securely fastened, the moment arrives to take that bold step off the platform. The initial seconds are a blur of wind and excitement as you soar through the air. The zipline propels you across the gorge, offering a bird's-eye view of the Niagara River below and the lush surroundings. The sensation of speed, combined with the natural beauty surrounding you, creates an adrenaline rush like no other.

Spectacular Scenery

As you glide through the open air, the gorge unfolds beneath you, revealing its rugged beauty and the sheer magnitude of the landscape. The roar of the falls echoes in the background, adding to the sensory experience. The zipline route is carefully designed to showcase the most breathtaking vantage points, ensuring that every moment is etched into your memory.

Expert Guidance

Safety is paramount during this adventure, and experienced guides accompany you every step of the way. They not only ensure that all safety protocols are followed but also share fascinating insights into the geology, history, and ecology of the gorge. Their expertise adds a layer of education to the adventure, making it both thrilling and informative.

Choosing the Right Zipline Experience

Niagara offers a variety of ziplining experiences catering to different preferences and comfort levels. Whether you opt for a solo ride or a tandem experience, each zipline promises a unique perspective and a rush of excitement. Some ziplines even offer a nighttime experience, allowing you to witness the falls illuminated under the moonlight—a truly magical and romantic adventure.

Capturing the Moment

Many ziplining operators provide opportunities to capture the adventure on camera. GoPros and other recording devices are often available to document your journey across the gorge, ensuring that you can relive the thrill and share the experience with friends and family.

Chapter 14: Winter Wonders

Frozen Falls: A Winter Wonderland

As the winter chill descends upon Niagara Falls, a magical transformation takes place, turning the iconic cascades into a breathtaking winter wonderland. The mist rising from the falls blankets the surrounding landscape in delicate layers of ice and snow, creating a scene straight out of a fairy tale.

Embracing the Frosty Splendor

The frozen falls offer a unique and enchanting experience for visitors willing to brave the cold. As you approach, you'll witness the falls adorned in a sparkling coat of ice, with delicate icicles hanging from the cliffs. The sound of rushing water is replaced by the mesmerizing crunch of snow underfoot, creating an otherworldly atmosphere.

Winter Activities by the Falls

Exploring the frozen falls opens up a realm of winter activities that add a dash of adventure to your visit. Strap on a pair of ice cleats and embark on a guided walking tour to get up close and personal with the icy masterpiece. Feel the chill on your face as you marvel at the surreal beauty of the frozen landscape, capturing Instagram-worthy moments at every turn.

For the more daring, ice climbing is a thrilling option. Expert guides lead you to the best climbing spots, ensuring a safe yet exhilarating ascent. Adrenaline courses through your veins as you conquer frozen cliffs with the falls as your backdrop—an experience that will stay with you long after the ice has melted.

Cozy Retreats and Warm Beverages

After a day of winter adventures, warm up in one of the many cozy retreats that dot the Niagara Falls area. Imagine sipping hot cocoa by a crackling fireplace, with panoramic views of the frozen falls through large windows. The local cafes and lodges offer the perfect refuge from the cold, creating a snug and inviting atmosphere for visitors to unwind.

For a truly immersive experience, consider a stay in a winter-themed cabin or lodge. Nestled in the snowy landscape, these accommodations provide a front-row seat to the frozen falls, allowing you to wake up to the magical sight of ice-covered cliffs and snow-covered trees.

Tips for Exploring Frozen Falls

Exploring the frozen falls requires some preparation to ensure a safe and enjoyable experience. Dress in layers to stay warm, and don't forget waterproof boots to navigate snowy paths. Joining a guided tour is recommended for those unfamiliar with winter conditions, as experienced guides provide insights into the natural wonders and ensure everyone's safety.

Whether you're an adventure seeker or someone who prefers to enjoy the winter wonder from a cozy vantage point, the frozen falls of Niagara offer a one-of-a-kind experience. Embrace the season's chill, and let the beauty of the icy landscape create memories that will linger in your heart long after the snow has melted away.

Ice Skating Near the Falls

When winter blankets the Niagara Falls region with a layer of snow and frost, a unique and enchanting experience awaits visitors: ice skating near the falls. The cold air, the sound of blades cutting through the ice, and the backdrop of the iconic falls create a winter wonderland that is both breathtaking and invigorating.

The Rink at Niagara Falls State Park

One of the prime locations for this frosty activity is The Rink at Niagara Falls State Park. Imagine gliding gracefully on the ice with the American and Horseshoe Falls as your backdrop. The rink is strategically located, offering skaters unparalleled views of the falls, especially when they are illuminated in the evening.

Open throughout the winter season, The Rink provides a perfect family-friendly atmosphere. Whether you're a novice or a seasoned skater, the rink caters to all skill levels. Rental skates are available, so you don't have to worry about bringing your own equipment.

Frosty Evenings and Dazzling Lights

One of the most magical aspects of ice skating near the falls is the combination of frosty evenings and the dazzling lights that illuminate the falls. As the sun sets and the falls are bathed in colorful lights, the entire experience takes on a fairytale-like quality.

Skating under the starry winter sky with the falls as a backdrop creates a romantic atmosphere, making it an ideal activity for couples looking to share a special moment. The sound of the falls adds a natural soundtrack to your skating adventure, making it an immersive and unforgettable experience.

Family Fun on Ice

For families, ice skating near the falls offers a wholesome winter activity. The laughter of children, the crisp winter air, and the joy of gliding on the ice create memories that last a lifetime. The open space around the rink allows for snowball fights and snowman building, adding an extra layer of winter fun.

Festive Atmosphere and Warm Treats

During the holiday season, the rink is often adorned with festive decorations, creating a cheerful and warm atmosphere. Visitors can enjoy hot cocoa and other winter treats at nearby concessions, adding to the overall festive experience. The scent of roasting chestnuts and the warmth of the seasonal beverages provide a cozy contrast to the chilly surroundings.

Tips for a Perfect Skating Experience

- Check the Weather: Before heading to the rink, check the weather conditions. Skating near the falls in a light snowfall can be a magical experience, but safety comes first.

- Bundle Up: Dress warmly in layers. The cold breeze from the falls can be chilly, even for the most enthusiastic skaters.

- Arrive Early: To make the most of your experience, arrive early to avoid crowds. Skating in the quieter hours allows for a more intimate connection with the natural beauty surrounding the rink.

Ice skating near the falls is not just a winter activity; it's a magical journey into the heart of winter's embrace, where nature and recreation come together to create an experience like no other. Lace up your skates and glide into the enchantment of a winter wonderland near the iconic Niagara Falls.

Cozy Winter Retreats

Winter around Niagara Falls transforms the landscape into a magical wonderland, and there's no better way to experience it than by indulging in cozy winter retreats. The region offers a range of charming accommodations that provide the perfect blend of comfort and winter charm.

Lakeside Cabins with Fireplace Warmth

Imagine waking up to the serene view of a snow-covered lake from the warmth of your cabin. Lakeside retreats around Niagara Falls offer an idyllic winter escape. Many cabins come equipped with rustic fireplaces, perfect for snuggling up with a cup of hot cocoa after a day of exploring the winter wonderland outside. The ambiance of a crackling fire and the soft glow of the flames create a truly enchanting atmosphere.

Bed-and-Breakfast Charm

For a more intimate and homey experience, consider staying in one of the charming bed-and-breakfast establishments nestled in the heart of the region. These cozy retreats often boast Victorian-era architecture, providing a quaint backdrop to your winter getaway. Picture yourself enjoying a homemade breakfast in a warmly decorated dining room before setting out to discover the frost-covered landscapes.

Spa Resorts for Winter Pampering

To truly unwind during the winter months, opt for a stay at one of the spa resorts in the area. These retreats not only offer luxurious accommodations but also provide a range of winter-themed spa treatments. Imagine soaking in a hot tub while surrounded by snow-covered trees or indulging in a massage that incorporates winter scents like pine and peppermint. It's a pampering experience that complements the natural beauty of the season.

Chalets with Mountain Views

For those seeking a touch of alpine charm, consider booking a stay in one of the mountain chalets near Niagara Falls. These cozy abodes often feature large windows that frame breathtaking views of snow-covered peaks. You can spend your days exploring nearby trails and then return to your chalet for a warm evening by the fire. It's a retreat that combines the tranquility of the mountains with the beauty of a winter landscape.

Culinary Escapes in Historic Inns

Winter retreats are not just about the scenery; they're also an opportunity to indulge in delicious winter cuisine. Historic inns in the area offer a unique blend of old-world charm and culinary delights. Picture yourself savoring hearty winter dishes by a roaring fireplace, with the history of the inn adding an extra layer of charm to your dining experience.

Chapter 15: Cultural Immersion

Indigenous Heritage Experiences

Niagara Falls isn't just a natural wonder; it's also a place rich in indigenous history and culture. As you explore the region, take the opportunity to immerse yourself in the traditions and stories of the First Nations people who have called this area home for centuries.

Discovering Indigenous Roots

Niagara Falls holds deep significance for the indigenous peoples of the region, particularly the Haudenosaunee (Iroquois) and Ojibwe nations. Begin your journey by visiting the Niagara Falls History Museum, where exhibits showcase the vibrant history and culture of these communities. Learn about their deep connection to the land, their spiritual beliefs, and the resilience of their traditions.

Traditional Performances and Art

To experience indigenous culture in a more dynamic way, attend traditional performances and art exhibitions. Many local venues and cultural centers host events featuring traditional dances, storytelling, and artwork. These performances not only entertain but also offer a profound insight into the spiritual and cultural significance of each dance or piece of art.

Guided Indigenous Tours

Enhance your understanding of the indigenous heritage by joining guided tours led by knowledgeable storytellers. These tours often take you to sacred sites, offering a unique perspective on the natural wonders of the area. Listen to legends and myths passed down through generations as you stand in the presence of the mighty falls, gaining a deeper appreciation for the spiritual connection between the indigenous people and the land.

Interactive Workshops

For a hands-on experience, participate in interactive workshops that showcase traditional indigenous crafts and skills. From beadwork to dreamcatcher weaving, these workshops provide a unique opportunity to learn directly from skilled artisans. Engaging in these activities fosters a sense of connection and respect for the cultural practices that have been preserved for centuries.

Supporting Indigenous Businesses

Take the time to explore indigenous-owned businesses in the Niagara Falls area. From art galleries featuring indigenous artists to shops selling handmade crafts, these establishments offer authentic and meaningful souvenirs. By supporting indigenous businesses, you contribute to the preservation of their culture and help sustain local communities.

Connecting with Indigenous Elders

If the opportunity arises, engage in conversations with indigenous elders who generously share their wisdom and stories. Their perspectives provide valuable insights into the history, challenges, and aspirations of their communities. Building these connections fosters mutual respect and a deeper appreciation for the diverse cultures that have shaped the Niagara Falls region.

In embracing indigenous heritage experiences at Niagara Falls, you not only enrich your own journey but also contribute to the preservation and celebration of the vibrant cultures that continue to thrive in this awe-inspiring landscape.

Art Galleries and Exhibitions

we dive into the vibrant world of art galleries and exhibitions that add a touch of creativity to the powerful landscape.

Indigenous Artistry:

Start your art journey by exploring the rich Indigenous heritage of the region. Several galleries showcase traditional and contemporary Indigenous art, providing a unique perspective on the cultural tapestry of the area. From intricate beadwork to stunning paintings, these exhibits offer a glimpse into the profound connection between the artists and their ancestral lands.

Contemporary Expressions:

Niagara Falls has a burgeoning contemporary art scene that reflects the dynamic spirit of the region. Local artists, inspired by the falls and the diverse community, contribute to galleries that celebrate innovation and individual expression. These exhibitions often rotate, ensuring there's always something new and thought-provoking to discover.

Interactive Installations:

Step beyond the traditional gallery experience with interactive installations that engage the senses. Some exhibits go beyond the visual, incorporating sound, touch, and even scent to create a multi-dimensional encounter with art. These immersive displays provide a unique opportunity to connect with the artwork on a more personal and visceral level.

Art Along the River:

Some galleries strategically position themselves along the river, allowing visitors to enjoy both the artistic creations and the natural beauty simultaneously. Imagine strolling through a gallery with panoramic views of the falls, creating a seamless blend of human creativity and Mother Nature's masterpiece.

Cultural Fusion Exhibitions:

Niagara Falls is a melting pot of cultures, and this is beautifully reflected in art exhibitions that celebrate diversity. These displays often feature collaborative works by artists from different backgrounds, showcasing the harmonious coexistence of various cultural influences within the community.

Art Walks and Festivals:

Embark on an art-centric journey with organized art walks and festivals. Local businesses and galleries often come together to create a vibrant atmosphere, where you can explore pop-up exhibits, street performances, and open-air galleries. These events not only support local artists but also create a lively and communal experience for art enthusiasts.

Educational Art Programs:

For those looking to delve deeper into the artistic realm, consider participating in educational programs offered by some galleries. Workshops, lectures, and classes provide valuable insights into different art forms, allowing visitors to develop a deeper appreciation for the creative process.

Public Art Installations:

Beyond gallery walls, Niagara Falls boasts an array of public art installations that add a touch of whimsy and inspiration to the urban landscape. From sculptures to murals, these outdoor artworks contribute to the open-air gallery experience, making art an integral part of the city's identity.

Art and Conservation:

Some galleries take a unique approach by combining art with environmental conservation themes. Exhibits may explore the intersection of art and nature, emphasizing the importance of preserving the natural beauty that serves as a backdrop to these creative endeavors.

Local Workshops and Classes

Beyond the thundering beauty of Niagara Falls, the region offers a diverse array of workshops and classes that provide a unique cultural immersion. Engaging in these activities allows visitors to connect with the community on a deeper level, gaining insights into local traditions and fostering a sense of creativity. Here are some exceptional workshops and classes to consider:

Indigenous Arts and Crafts Workshops

Immerse yourself in the rich heritage of the indigenous peoples of the region by participating in arts and crafts workshops. Led by skilled artisans, these sessions provide hands-on experiences in traditional practices such as beadwork, dreamcatcher crafting, and storytelling. Participants not only create their own unique pieces but also gain a profound appreciation for the cultural significance of each art form.

Niagara Culinary Classes

For those with a passion for food, Niagara offers culinary classes that delve into the region's bountiful local produce. Learn the art of wine pairing with Niagara wines, discover the secrets of crafting the perfect maple syrup, or join cooking classes that showcase the diverse flavors of the area. These classes not only tantalize the taste buds but also offer a glimpse into the culinary traditions that have evolved in this vibrant locale.

Photography Workshops with Local Artists

Capture the breathtaking landscapes of Niagara Falls through the lens by enrolling in photography workshops led by local artists. These professionals not only guide participants in mastering their camera skills but also share their unique perspectives on capturing the essence of the falls and surrounding areas. The workshops often include both classroom sessions and practical, on-location shooting, providing a comprehensive learning experience for photography enthusiasts.

Niagara History Lectures

Delve into the rich history of the Niagara region through engaging history lectures conducted by local experts. These classes cover a wide range of topics, from the geological formation of the falls to the fascinating stories of the people who have called this area home. History enthusiasts can deepen their understanding of the region's past, gaining insights that enhance their overall experience of Niagara.

Nature Sketching and Painting

Unleash your creative spirit amid the natural beauty of Niagara with nature sketching and painting classes. Taught by local artists, these sessions encourage participants to find inspiration in the lush landscapes, serene waterways, and vibrant flora surrounding the falls. Whether you are a seasoned artist or a beginner, these classes provide a serene and inspiring environment to express your creativity.

Participating in local workshops and classes adds an enriching layer to your Niagara Falls adventure, allowing you to take home not only memories of the stunning natural wonder but also newfound skills and insights into the cultural tapestry of this remarkable region.

Chapter 16: Eco-Friendly Explorations

Nature Reserves and Parks

we'll delve into the captivating world of nature reserves and parks surrounding the Niagara Falls region, offering a sanctuary for those who crave a break from the bustling energy of the falls.

Exploring Niagara's Natural Treasures

1. Niagara Glen Nature Reserve: Tucked away along the Niagara River, the Niagara Glen Nature Reserve stands as a testament to the region's geological history. Venture along the well-marked trails to discover ancient rock formations, diverse flora, and a vibrant ecosystem. The Whirlpool Aero Car, offering panoramic views, adds an extra layer of excitement to your nature escape.

2. Queenston Heights Park: Rich in history and natural beauty, Queenston Heights Park is a must-visit for those seeking a tranquil escape. The park boasts well-maintained gardens, hiking trails, and the iconic Brock's Monument, commemorating the War of 1812. Take a leisurely stroll, breathe in the fragrant air, and absorb the serene ambiance that permeates the park.

3. Dufferin Islands: Just south of the falls, Dufferin Islands offers a secluded retreat surrounded by water and lush greenery. A network of interconnected islands linked by picturesque bridges creates an enchanting landscape. It's a perfect spot for birdwatching, with a variety of migratory birds making a stopover during their journeys.
Conservation and Sustainability

Niagara's commitment to preserving its natural treasures is evident in the various conservation initiatives undertaken in these reserves and parks. Efforts are made to maintain the delicate balance of the ecosystem, ensuring that future generations can also revel in the beauty of the region.

1. Sustainable Practices: Many of these nature reserves adhere to sustainable practices, such as eco-friendly trail maintenance and waste reduction programs. Visitors are encouraged to follow Leave No Trace principles, minimizing their impact on the environment.

2. Educational Programs: Nature reserves often host educational programs to raise awareness about the local ecology and wildlife. Guided tours, interactive exhibits, and workshops provide visitors with valuable insights into the importance of conservation.

Activities for Nature Enthusiasts

1. Hiking Adventures: Lace up your hiking boots and explore the numerous trails that wind through these reserves. From easy walks suitable for families to more challenging routes for seasoned hikers, there's a path for everyone.

2. Birdwatching: Niagara's parks are a haven for birdwatchers. Grab your binoculars and spot a diverse array of bird species, from majestic raptors soaring in the sky to delicate songbirds nestled in the trees.

3. Photography Opportunities: Nature reserves and parks offer a plethora of scenic views and photo-worthy moments. Capture the vibrant colors of the flora, the serenity of winding trails, and the playfulness of wildlife in their natural habitat.

Planning Your Nature Escape

Before embarking on your nature adventure, it's advisable to check the park or reserve's official website for any seasonal closures, trail conditions, or special events. Whether you're a solo traveler seeking solitude or a family looking for outdoor activities, Niagara's nature reserves and parks provide a diverse range of experiences to suit every nature lover's preference.

In the heart of this iconic tourist destination, these natural sanctuaries stand as a testament to the importance of preserving and celebrating the environment. Immerse yourself in the tranquility, marvel at the biodiversity, and discover a side of Niagara that goes beyond the thunderous roar of its famous falls.

Bird Watching by the Falls

Embarking on a bird-watching adventure by the Falls offers a unique blend of natural beauty and avian wonder. As the majestic Niagara Falls roars in the background, bird enthusiasts can immerse themselves in a serene and picturesque environment that attracts a diverse range of bird species.

The Ideal Spots for Bird Watching

Niagara Falls State Park provides an ideal vantage point for bird watching. With its expansive greenery and proximity to the falls, the park becomes a haven for various bird species. The lush vegetation, including trees and shrubs, creates an inviting habitat for both migratory and resident birds.

One of the highlights of bird watching near Niagara Falls is the opportunity to spot water-loving birds. The mist rising from the falls provides a unique microclimate, making it an attractive spot for waterfowl. Visitors can often observe ducks, geese, and even elegant swans gracefully gliding on the ponds and rivers surrounding the falls.

Migratory Marvels

Niagara Falls serves as a crucial stopover for many migratory birds during their long journeys. The Niagara River corridor acts as a natural migratory pathway, and bird watchers can witness the spectacular sight of various species in flight. Spring and fall are particularly exciting seasons as warblers, hawks, and other migratory birds traverse the region.

Bird watchers should keep their binoculars ready for the incredible aerial displays of birds of prey. Hawks, eagles, and falcons are known to soar above the falls, taking advantage of the rising air currents. These skilled fliers provide a breathtaking spectacle against the backdrop of the cascading waters.

Tips for Bird Watching Success

For a rewarding bird-watching experience, consider the following tips:

- Binoculars and Field Guide: Bring a pair of quality binoculars to observe birds up close. A field guide specific to the region's bird species can help in identification.

- Early Mornings and Late Afternoons: Birds are most active during these times, making them optimal for bird watching. The soft sunlight also enhances the visual experience.

- Patience is Key: Bird watching requires patience. Find a comfortable spot, settle in, and allow the birds to reveal themselves in their natural habitat.

- Respect Nature: Keep a respectful distance from the birds and their nests to avoid causing unnecessary stress to the wildlife.

Conservation Efforts

Niagara Falls, with its unique ecosystem, underscores the importance of conservation efforts. Bird watching enthusiasts can contribute to these efforts by supporting local conservation initiatives and being mindful of the impact of human activities on the natural habitat.

Chapter 17: Romance by the Falls

Romantic Dining Spots

When it comes to creating memorable moments with your loved one, the dining experience plays a crucial role. Here, we explore some of the most romantic dining spots that offer not just delectable cuisine but also a captivating atmosphere.

The Keg Steakhouse + Bar

Located on the ninth floor of the Embassy Suites by Hilton Niagara Falls Fallsview, The Keg Steakhouse + Bar boasts stunning panoramic views of both the American and Horseshoe Falls. Imagine savoring a perfectly cooked steak while surrounded by the soft glow of city lights and the thunderous sound of the falls in the background. The intimate ambiance and impeccable service make this spot a favorite among couples seeking a romantic evening.

Windows by Jamie Kennedy Fresh Grill & Wine Bar

Perched atop the Sheraton on the Falls hotel, Windows by Jamie Kennedy Fresh Grill & Wine Bar offers a dining experience that combines gourmet cuisine with a spectacular view. The floor-to-ceiling windows provide an uninterrupted sight of the falls, creating an intimate setting for a romantic dinner. The menu, curated by renowned chef Jamie Kennedy, features locally sourced ingredients, adding a touch of freshness to every dish.

Queen Victoria Place Restaurant

For couples who appreciate history and charm, the Queen Victoria Place Restaurant is an ideal choice. Situated in a historic building in Queen Victoria Park, this restaurant offers a refined atmosphere with both indoor and outdoor seating options. Enjoy a candlelit dinner on the terrace overlooking the beautifully manicured gardens, with the falls as a breathtaking backdrop. The menu features a mix of classic and contemporary dishes prepared with a focus on locally sourced ingredients.

Peller Estates Winery Restaurant

Wine and romance often go hand in hand, and Peller Estates Winery Restaurant takes this pairing to a whole new level. Nestled in the heart of wine country, this restaurant offers a vineyard-to-table dining experience. The ambiance is both elegant and cozy, with warm wood accents and a fireplace. The menu, designed to complement Peller Estates' award-winning wines, showcases the best of Niagara's culinary offerings.

Watermark Restaurant

Perched on the 33rd floor of the Hilton Hotel and Suites, the Watermark Restaurant offers a sophisticated dining experience with a modern twist. The revolving dining room provides 360-degree views of the falls and the surrounding landscape. As you enjoy your meal, the ever-changing scenery becomes a mesmerizing backdrop, creating an unforgettable romantic atmosphere.

Sunset Cruises

Embark on a journey where nature's most breathtaking spectacle unfolds—the sunset over Niagara Falls. Sunset

Cruises offer an unrivaled front-row seat to witness the sky transform into a canvas of warm tones. As the boat glides gently on the water, passengers are treated to a symphony of colors, with the falls providing a majestic backdrop to this natural spectacle.

The Perfect Setting for Romance:
Sunset Cruises are inherently romantic, providing couples with an intimate and picturesque setting. Imagine sipping on champagne or a signature cocktail as you share quiet moments with your loved one, surrounded by the beauty of the falls bathed in the warm glow of the setting sun. Many cruise operators design these experiences with romance in mind, offering cozy seating, soft music, and attentive service.

Variety of Cruise Options:
From large vessels to more private and intimate sailings, Sunset Cruises cater to diverse preferences. Some cruises include dinner options, allowing couples to indulge in a sumptuous meal while the sun bids its daily farewell. Others may opt for smaller boats, creating an exclusive and personal atmosphere for a truly romantic escape.

Exclusive Views:
One of the key advantages of a Sunset Cruise is the exclusive vantage point it provides. As the boat navigates the water, you'll witness the falls in a way that land-based spectators can only dream of. The changing hues of the falls, coupled with the play of light and shadow, create a mesmerizing scene that is both unique and unforgettable.

Photographic Opportunities:
For those with a penchant for photography, a Sunset Cruise is a golden opportunity to capture the falls in all their evening glory. The reflections on the water, the silhouettes against the darkening sky, and the occasional mist rising

from the falls create a dreamlike panorama that is a photographer's delight.
Tips for the Perfect Sunset Cruise:

- Timing is Everything: Check the timing of the sunset and choose a cruise that aligns with this magical moment.
- Dress Comfortably: Evenings near the falls can get cool, so bring a light jacket or shawl to stay comfortable.
- Book in Advance: Sunset Cruises are popular, especially during peak seasons. Secure your spot by booking in advance.

A Sunset Cruise near Niagara Falls is not merely a boat ride; it's an experience that lingers in the hearts of those who partake in its beauty. Whether celebrating a special occasion or simply reveling in each other's company, this chapter invites couples to immerse themselves in the romance that unfolds when the sun bids adieu to the magnificent Niagara Falls.

Enchanting Proposal Locations

Choosing the perfect location to propose is a momentous task. Niagara Falls, with its breathtaking beauty, offers a myriad of enchanting spots that are sure to make your proposal a memory to cherish forever.

Moonlit Stroll on the Rainbow Bridge

Imagine walking hand in hand under the soft glow of the moon on the iconic Rainbow Bridge. As you approach the middle, with the falls illuminated in the background, it creates a magical ambiance. The sound of rushing water below and the city lights in the distance add a touch of romance that makes it an ideal spot for a moonlit proposal.

Private Gazebo at Queen Victoria Park

Queen Victoria Park is renowned for its stunning floral displays and manicured lawns, but hidden within its beauty are secluded gazebos that provide a private and intimate setting. Set against the backdrop of the falls, these gazebos offer a perfect blend of nature and tranquility—ideal for a heartfelt proposal surrounded by blooming flowers and the sound of cascading water.

Fireworks Over the Falls

Timing is everything, and if you plan your proposal during one of Niagara Falls' spectacular fireworks displays, you'll be adding an extra layer of magic. Imagine getting down on one knee as the night sky is ablaze with colors, mirroring the love and excitement of the moment. Opt for a spot with a panoramic view, perhaps from a cozy rooftop restaurant or a scenic overlook.

Boat Proposal with Hornblower Cruises

For a unique and adventurous proposal, consider popping the question aboard a Hornblower Cruise. Feel the mist of the falls on your face as you ask that special question against the backdrop of the illuminated cascades. The boat's gentle sway and the falls' thundering roar provide a dramatic setting that is sure to sweep your partner off their feet.

Secret Garden at Oakes Garden Theatre

Tucked away within Niagara Falls' Oakes Garden Theatre is a hidden gem—a secret garden that feels like a slice of paradise. With its winding paths, lush greenery, and blooming flowers, this secluded spot exudes romance. Choose a quiet bench or a charming gazebo to make your proposal amidst the serene beauty of the garden.

Candlelit Dinner at Skylon Tower's Revolving Dining Room

Elevate your proposal to new heights—literally. The Revolving Dining Room at Skylon Tower offers panoramic views of the falls and the surrounding landscape. Plan a candlelit dinner with a window-side table, and as you enjoy your meal, let the slow rotation of the room create a cinematic backdrop for your romantic moment.

Sunrise at Horseshoe Falls

For early birds in love, a sunrise proposal at Horseshoe Falls is a captivating choice. The soft hues of dawn, the quiet surroundings, and the first light kissing the mist create a tranquil and ethereal atmosphere. Capture the beginning of a new day and a new chapter in your lives against the world-famous falls.

Chapter 18: Haunted Niagara

Ghost Tours and Legends

As the sun sets and darkness blankets the landscape, embark on an eerie journey into the supernatural with the ghost tours and legends that abound in the region.

Ghost Tours:

One of the most spine-tingling ways to experience the haunted history of Niagara is by joining a ghost tour. Professional guides lead you through dimly lit paths and historic sites, sharing tales of spirits that are said to linger in the misty air. The tours often include visits to haunted hotels, abandoned buildings, and locations with a reputation for paranormal activity.

Imagine walking along the Niagara Parkway, guided only by the dim glow of lanterns, as your guide recounts chilling stories of apparitions seen near the rushing waters. These tours not only provide a glimpse into the supernatural but also offer a unique perspective on the rich history of the area.

Legends of the Mist:

Niagara Falls has inspired countless legends, some of which have taken on a spectral quality over the years. One such legend is that of the Maid of the Mist, a Native American woman who, heartbroken over a lost love, is said to appear as a misty figure near the falls. Locals and visitors alike have reported glimpses of her ethereal presence, adding a layer of mystique to the already enchanting surroundings.

Another tale involves the tragic love story of a daredevil who attempted to conquer the falls in a barrel. Though the attempt ended fatally, some claim to hear echoes of his restless spirit in the roar of the cascading water. These legends, passed down through generations, contribute to the haunted allure of Niagara Falls.

Paranormal Experiences:

For those seeking a more immersive encounter with the supernatural, Niagara offers paranormal experiences that go beyond traditional ghost tours. Haunted overnight stays in historic inns and hotels, known for their spectral inhabitants, provide an opportunity to connect with the otherworldly.

Imagine spending a night in a room with a reputation for unexplained phenomena—flickering lights, mysterious sounds, and subtle movements that defy logical explanation. Paranormal investigators often lead these experiences, equipped with tools to detect and document any signs of ghostly activity.

As you delve into the ghostly side of Niagara, keep in mind that whether you're a skeptic or a believer, the stories and experiences shared on these tours and encounters are sure to leave a lasting impression. Haunted Niagara is not just a collection of spooky tales but a journey into the unknown, where the line between reality and the supernatural becomes delightfully blurred. So, as the shadows lengthen and the falls echo with the legends of the mist, dare to explore the haunted side of this iconic destination.

Spooky Sites to Explore

Niagara Falls has a darker side—an undercurrent of paranormal activity that adds a thrilling edge to the experience. we will explore some of the haunted sites that have become the stuff of local legends and ghostly tales.

Old Fort Niagara: The Ghosts of History

Nestled at the mouth of the Niagara River, Old Fort Niagara stands as a silent witness to centuries of history. This military outpost, dating back to the 18th century, has seen its share of conflicts and tragedies. Many believe that the spirits of soldiers and prisoners from bygone eras still roam its grounds.

Visitors to Old Fort Niagara have reported eerie encounters such as mysterious footsteps, unexplained whispers, and sightings of shadowy figures. The dungeons, where prisoners faced harsh conditions, are said to be particularly active with paranormal energy. Ghost tours are offered for those daring enough to explore the fort after dark, providing a spine-chilling journey through history.

Screaming Tunnel: A Haunting Legend

Venture just outside Niagara Falls to the infamous Screaming Tunnel, a seemingly peaceful passageway with a macabre tale. According to local legend, the tunnel is haunted by the spirit of a young girl who met a tragic end. It is said that if you ignite a match in the middle of the tunnel, you may hear her blood-curdling scream.

The story varies, with some accounts suggesting the girl was escaping a fire while others claim a darker tale of violence. Regardless, the Screaming Tunnel has become a magnet for ghost hunters and thrill-seekers eager to test the legend. The atmosphere inside the tunnel, especially at night, is heavy with an unexplained sense of foreboding.

Drummond Hill Cemetery: Where History Meets the Supernatural

Cemeteries often hold stories of the departed, but Drummond Hill Cemetery takes it a step further. This historic burial ground, dating back to the War of 1812, is not only a repository of local history but also a reputed hotspot for paranormal activity.

Among the gravestones and aged monuments, visitors have reported ghostly apparitions and strange phenomena. Some claim to have seen soldiers in tattered uniforms, while others have felt an inexplicable chill in the air. With its combination of history and hauntings, Drummond Hill Cemetery offers a unique and spine-tingling journey through time.

As you explore these spooky sites around Niagara Falls, remember to approach with a mix of curiosity and respect. Whether you're a skeptic or a believer, the haunted history of these locations adds a layer of intrigue to the region's rich tapestry of stories. Who knows, you might just have your own ghostly encounter amidst the beauty of Niagara's darker side.

Paranormal Experiences

If you're a thrill-seeker with a penchant for the paranormal, this chapter is your guide to the spookier side of the falls. Brace yourself as we delve into the mysterious and haunted sites that lurk in the shadows of this iconic destination.

1. The Screaming Tunnel:

Nestled just outside Niagara Falls, the Screaming Tunnel has a haunting reputation. Legend has it that the tunnel is haunted by the ghost of a young girl who met a tragic end within its cold, stone walls. Brave souls venture here to test their mettle by lighting a match in the middle of the tunnel, only to have it extinguished by an unseen force.

2. Drummond Hill Cemetery:

Cemeteries have long been associated with ghostly apparitions, and Drummond Hill Cemetery is no exception. Dating back to the War of 1812, this cemetery is said to be haunted by soldiers who lost their lives in battle. Eerie sightings and unexplained phenomena have been reported by visitors who wander through the gravestones.

3. Old Fort Erie:

With a history steeped in warfare and tragedy, Old Fort Erie is not only a historical site but also a rumored hub for paranormal activity. Visitors have reported ghostly sightings of soldiers in uniform and the sounds of phantom battles echoing through the aged corridors.

4. The Blue Ghost Tunnel:

This abandoned railway tunnel, also known as the Merritton Tunnel, has gained notoriety for its ghostly encounters. The legend revolves around workers who lost their lives during its construction, and their spirits are said to linger within the tunnel. Those who dare to explore often recount unsettling experiences, from strange whispers to unexplained apparitions.

5. The Angel Inn:

A historic pub in the town of Niagara-on-the-Lake, The Angel Inn has a reputation for being haunted by the spirits of soldiers from the War of 1812. Guests have reported ghostly figures, mysterious footsteps, and the clinking of glasses in empty rooms, creating an atmosphere that sends shivers down the spine.

6. McFarland House:

This charming 19th-century house in Niagara-on-the-Lake is rumored to be haunted by the ghost of a former owner. Visitors have reported encountering the apparition of a lady in white, believed to be the spirit of Grace McFarland, who tragically lost her life in the house.

Exploring these spooky sites around Niagara Falls offers a unique blend of history and the supernatural. Whether you're a skeptic or a true believer, the eerie tales and haunted locales add an extra layer of intrigue to this already captivating region. So, if you dare, venture into the shadows and unlock the mysteries that linger in the ghostly corners of Niagara Falls.

Chapter 19: Waterfront Relaxation

Lakeside Retreats

Niagara Falls isn't just about the breathtaking cascade of water; it's also surrounded by serene lakeside retreats that offer a perfect escape from the hustle and bustle. Whether you're seeking solitude, a romantic getaway, or a family vacation, these lakeside retreats near Niagara Falls provide a tranquil haven.

1. Tranquil Waterside Cabins

Imagine waking up to the gentle lapping of waves against the shore. Lakeside cabins offer just that, providing a cozy and intimate escape from the everyday grind. Nestled along the shores of Lake Ontario or Lake Erie, these cabins often come equipped with private docks, allowing guests to bask in the tranquility of the water at any time of day.

2. Sunset Views from Lakeside Resorts

For those who appreciate the finer things in life, lakeside resorts near Niagara Falls boast stunning views of the setting sun over the water. Picture yourself sipping a glass of local wine on a balcony overlooking the lake, the sky ablaze with hues of orange and pink. These resorts often feature luxurious amenities, including spa services and gourmet dining experiences.

3. Waterfront Campsites for Nature Enthusiasts

If you're more of an outdoor enthusiast, lakeside campsites offer a unique experience. Set up your tent along the shores of Lake Ontario or Lake Erie and fall asleep to the soothing sounds of nature. Wake up to the sunrise dancing on the water, and spend your days exploring nearby trails or enjoying water activities.

4. Lakeside Bed and Breakfasts

For a charming and personalized lakeside experience, consider staying at a bed and breakfast by the lake. Hosts often provide insider tips on the best lakeside activities and local hidden gems. Wake up to a homemade breakfast and step outside to enjoy the peaceful surroundings.

5. Lakeside Activities for All Ages

These retreats aren't just about relaxation—they offer a plethora of lakeside activities. From kayaking and paddleboarding to fishing off the dock, there's something for everyone. Families can bond over lakeside picnics, and couples can take romantic sunset strolls along the water's edge.

6. Seasonal Beauty Year-Round

Each season brings its own charm to the lakeside retreats. In the summer, enjoy water-based activities and vibrant green landscapes. Fall paints the shores in warm hues, creating a picturesque scene. Winter blankets the retreats in a serene quietude, and spring brings the rebirth of nature.

Fishing Adventures

The diverse aquatic ecosystems surrounding the falls provide a rich habitat for various fish species, making it an ideal destination for those who appreciate the art of angling.

The Niagara River's Bounty

The Niagara River, a vital waterway connecting Lake Erie to Lake Ontario, is the primary stage for these fishing adventures. Known for its strong currents and deep pools, the river attracts an array of fish, including bass, walleye, trout, and salmon. Anglers can cast their lines from the riverbanks or embark on fishing charters for a more immersive experience.

Seasonal Fishing Delights

The fishing experience varies with the seasons, offering a year-round appeal to enthusiasts. Spring and fall are particularly popular, as salmon and trout migrations create a fishing frenzy. Summer brings opportunities for bass and walleye fishing, while winter transforms the area into an ice fishing paradise. Each season offers a distinct charm, ensuring that anglers can find excitement regardless of when they visit.

Guided Fishing Charters

For those seeking a more guided experience, numerous fishing charters operate in the region. Experienced local guides lead participants to the best fishing spots, sharing their knowledge of the area and providing valuable tips. Charter trips not only enhance the chances of a successful catch but also offer a unique perspective of the Niagara River and its surrounding landscapes.

Fishing Equipment and Rentals

Visitors need not worry about bringing their own equipment, as several outfitters and rental services cater to anglers of all levels. From basic fishing gear to specialized equipment for specific species, these services ensure that everyone can partake in the joys of fishing without the need for an extensive personal setup.

Scenic Spots for Shore Fishing

For those who prefer the simplicity of shore fishing, there are plenty of picturesque spots along the riverbanks. Parks and designated fishing areas provide a peaceful setting, allowing anglers to cast their lines against the backdrop of the rushing waters and lush landscapes. It's not just about the catch; it's about the experience of communing with nature in one of the most beautiful settings in the world.

Conservation Efforts

Niagara's fishing community is deeply committed to sustainability and conservation. Catch-and-release practices are encouraged for certain species to maintain the delicate balance of the ecosystem. Anglers are not just participants in the sport; they are stewards of the environment, ensuring that future generations can continue to enjoy the thrill of fishing in these pristine waters.

Picnic Spots with a View

When it comes to enjoying a peaceful day surrounded by natural beauty, few activities rival the simplicity and charm of a picnic. In the Niagara Falls region, there are enchanting picnic spots that offer not only a serene atmosphere but also breathtaking views that elevate your outdoor dining experience.

1. Queen Victoria Park

Nestled on the Canadian side of the falls, Queen Victoria Park stands as a premier destination for a picturesque picnic. With manicured lawns, vibrant flower displays, and strategically placed benches, it provides an idyllic setting for a leisurely afternoon. Spread out your blanket and savor your meal as you overlook the powerful Niagara Falls, feeling the mist on your face and listening to the thundering roar of the cascading waters.

2. Three Sisters Islands

For a more secluded picnic, venture to Three Sisters Islands on Goat Island. Accessible via a scenic walking trail, these islands offer a quiet retreat from the bustling crowds. Find a spot along the river's edge, surrounded by lush greenery and the soothing sounds of the water flowing around the islands. It's a perfect location for couples seeking a romantic picnic spot with an intimate ambiance.

3. Niagara Glen Nature Reserve

If you're a nature enthusiast, the Niagara Glen Nature Reserve provides a unique picnic experience. Set amidst a rugged gorge, this reserve features marked trails that lead to rocky outcrops overlooking the Niagara River. Choose a spot on the grassy banks, and enjoy your picnic while immersed in the natural beauty of the surrounding forests and cliffs.

4. Oakes Garden Theatre

For those with a penchant for horticulture, Oakes Garden Theatre is a must-visit. This meticulously landscaped garden offers an elegant backdrop for your picnic, with its ornate floral arrangements and sculpted hedges. Enjoy your meal surrounded by the artistic beauty of the gardens while relishing the views of the American Falls and Bridal Veil Falls.

5. Fort Niagara State Park

Crossing over to the American side, Fort Niagara State Park provides a spacious and scenic setting for a family picnic. Spread out on the expansive lawns overlooking Lake Ontario and the mouth of the Niagara River. After your meal, explore the historic fort and its surroundings, adding a touch of education to your day of relaxation.

6. Dufferin Islands

For a magical and secluded experience, head to Dufferin Islands, a hidden gem located just south of the falls. These interconnected islands are adorned with walking paths, bridges, and serene ponds. Choose a spot along the water's edge and revel in the tranquility of this secret oasis while enjoying your picnic fare.

In these enchanting picnic spots, the combination of delectable food, natural beauty, and awe-inspiring views creates an unforgettable experience. Whether you're seeking romance, solitude, or a family-friendly outing, these waterfront picnic spots near Niagara Falls offer the perfect blend of relaxation and visual splendor. So, pack your basket, grab a blanket, and embark on a delightful journey of flavors and scenery in the heart of this natural wonder.

Chapter 20: Travel Itinerary

Family Friendly Itinerary

When planning a visit to the awe-inspiring Niagara Falls, a region renowned for its natural beauty and outdoor wonders, embracing the spirit of adventure is a must. This detailed itinerary spans several days, each packed with exhilarating activities that promise an unforgettable experience.

Day 1: Welcome to Niagara

Morning:

- Breakfast with a View at Skylon Tower: Start your day by indulging in a delicious breakfast at the Skylon Tower's revolving dining room. Enjoy panoramic views of the falls and surrounding landscapes.

Late Morning:

- Journey Behind the Falls: Head to Table Rock Centre and embark on the Journey Behind the Falls. Descend to the observation deck through tunnels and witness the sheer power and majesty of the falls from behind.

Afternoon:

- Whirlpool Aero Car: After a hearty lunch, head to the Whirlpool Aero Car. Soar over the Niagara Whirlpool and rapids in a cable car, providing a unique perspective of the Niagara River.

Evening:

- Dinner at Queenston Heights Restaurant: Conclude your day with a scenic drive to Queenston Heights. Enjoy dinner at the Queenston Heights Restaurant, surrounded by beautifully landscaped gardens.

Day 2: Adrenaline and Exploration

Morning:

- Jet Boat Adventure: Start your day with an adrenaline rush by taking a jet boat tour. Traverse the turbulent waters of the Niagara River, getting up close and personal with Class 5 rapids.

Late Morning:

- Ziplining Over the Gorge: Head to the Niagara Falls Zipline to experience the thrill of soaring over the gorge. Enjoy breathtaking views as you zip across the landscape.

Afternoon:

- Lunch at Clifton Hill: Recharge with a casual lunch at one of the eateries on Clifton Hill, the bustling entertainment district. Take a stroll and explore the vibrant attractions and souvenir shops.

Evening:

- Nighttime Illumination Cruise: As the sun sets, embark on a cruise to witness the falls illuminated in a stunning array of colors. Capture the mesmerizing views while cruising the Niagara River.

Day 3: Nature and Tranquility

Morning:

- Hiking in Niagara Glen: Start your day with a nature hike in the Niagara Glen Nature Reserve. Explore marked trails that lead to scenic viewpoints, offering a unique perspective of the river and gorge.

Late Morning:

- Picnic at Dufferin Islands: Enjoy a peaceful mid-morning picnic at Dufferin Islands. Surrounded by interconnected islands and serene ponds, it's a tranquil escape from the bustling tourist areas.

Afternoon:

- Winery Tour in Niagara-on-the-Lake: Head to the picturesque town of Niagara-on-the-Lake for a wine tour. Explore local vineyards, sample exquisite wines, and savor a gourmet lunch.

Evening:

- Sunset at Fort Niagara State Park: Cross the border for a serene evening at Fort Niagara State Park. Witness a captivating sunset over Lake Ontario, offering a different perspective of the Niagara region.

Day 4: Beyond the Falls

Morning:

- Morning Bike Ride along the Niagara Parkway: Rent bikes and explore the scenic Niagara Parkway. Enjoy the breathtaking views of the falls, river, and surrounding landscapes.

Late Morning:

- Exploring Niagara Parks Butterfly Conservatory: Immerse yourself in the vibrant world of butterflies at the Butterfly Conservatory. Wander through lush gardens and marvel at the diverse butterfly species.

Afternoon:

- Lunch at Niagara Falls Culinary Institute: Indulge in a culinary experience at the Niagara Falls Culinary Institute. Enjoy a gourmet lunch prepared by talented chefs.

Evening:

- Casino Night: Conclude your adventure with an evening of entertainment at one of the Niagara Falls casinos. Try your luck at the tables or enjoy a live show.

Day 5: Reflection and Departure

Morning:

- MistRider Zipline to the Falls: Start your final day with a thrilling zipline experience. Soar over the falls and feel the mist as you descend towards the landing platform.

Late Morning:

- White-Water Walk: Explore the White-Water Walk attraction, offering a close-up view of the powerful rapids. Walk along the boardwalk and marvel at the turbulent waters.

Afternoon:

- Farewell Lunch at Elements on the Falls: Enjoy a farewell lunch at Elements on the Falls. Relish the last moments with a meal overlooking the cascading falls.

Evening:

- Maid of the Mist Evening Cruise: Conclude your Niagara adventure with the iconic Maid of the Mist Evening Cruise. Experience the falls in a new light as they are bathed in the golden hues of the setting sun.

This comprehensive five-day outdoor adventure itinerary ensures that every moment spent at Niagara Falls is filled with excitement, natural beauty, and unforgettable experiences. From heart-pounding activities to tranquil nature retreats, this itinerary captures the essence of Niagara's diverse offerings.

Art and Culture Itinerary

When visiting Niagara Falls, it's easy to be captivated by the natural beauty of the cascading waters. However, the region is not only a feast for the eyes in terms of landscapes but also a hub of vibrant art and culture. Embark on a multi-day itinerary to delve into the artistic and cultural treasures that enrich the Niagara Falls experience.

Day 1: Discovering Local Art Galleries

Morning: Start at the Niagara Falls Art Gallery
Begin your cultural journey at the Niagara Falls Art Gallery, showcasing a diverse collection of contemporary and traditional art. Explore the exhibitions featuring local and international artists, and perhaps catch an interactive workshop or guided tour.

Afternoon: Stroll through Old Town
After a delightful morning, take a stroll through the historic Old Town. Admire the charming architecture and stop by the local boutiques and art shops. Don't miss the Niagara Pumphouse Arts Centre, a heritage building converted into a vibrant arts space with rotating exhibitions.

Evening: Cultural Cuisine at Queen Street

Wrap up your day with dinner at one of the culturally rich restaurants along Queen Street. Many eateries in this area not only serve delicious meals but also showcase local artworks. It's a perfect way to combine culinary delights with artistic appreciation.

Day 2: Immersing in Indigenous Heritage

Morning: Visit the Niagara Falls History Museum
Begin your day with a visit to the Niagara Falls History Museum. Gain insights into the region's rich history, including its Indigenous heritage. The museum often hosts exhibitions highlighting the art and culture of the First Nations people.

Afternoon: Journey to the Native Centre
Continue your exploration of Indigenous culture by visiting the Native Centre. Engage in interactive exhibits, traditional

storytelling, and perhaps participate in a craft workshop led by Indigenous artisans.

Evening: Indigenous Cuisine Experience
Cap off the day with a dinner experience featuring Indigenous cuisine. Several restaurants in the area offer dishes inspired by traditional Indigenous recipes, providing not only a flavorful meal but also a cultural immersion.

Day 3: A Day of Performing Arts

Morning: Behind the Scenes at Shaw Festival Theatre
Start your day with a behind-the-scenes tour at the Shaw Festival Theatre in nearby Niagara-on-the-Lake. Gain insights into the world of theatre production, and if timing aligns, catch a matinee performance.

Afternoon: Explore the Cultural District
Take the afternoon to explore the Cultural District around Queen Street and Victoria Avenue. Visit the Niagara Falls Cultural Centre, home to various performing arts groups and studios. Attend a dance or music rehearsal or peruse the galleries featuring local artists.

Evening: Dinner and a Show
End your day with a delightful dinner at a restaurant in the Cultural District, followed by a live performance. Whether it's a theatrical play, a musical concert, or a dance performance, Niagara Falls' vibrant arts scene has something to offer every night.

Day 4: Artistic Escapades in Nature

Morning: Artistic Trails at Lundy's Lane
Embark on a morning exploration of the artistic trails along Lundy's Lane. This area is adorned with outdoor sculptures

and murals, creating an open-air art gallery. Take a leisurely walk, appreciating the fusion of art and nature.

Afternoon: Wine and Art at Twenty Valley
Head to Twenty Valley, a short drive from Niagara Falls, known for its wineries. Enjoy a wine tasting experience paired with art exhibitions at select vineyards. It's a unique fusion of the region's two great passions – wine and art.

Evening: Sunset at the Botanical Gardens
Conclude your artistic escapades with a visit to the Niagara Parks Botanical Gardens. As the sun sets, the gardens come alive with special light installations and performances. It's a serene and enchanting way to wrap up your cultural exploration of Niagara Falls.

Day 5: Interactive Workshops and Local Artisans

Morning: Hands-On Workshop at Rodman Hall Art Centre
Start your day with a hands-on workshop at Rodman Hall Art Centre. Engage in painting, sculpture, or any other artistic endeavor guided by local artists. It's an opportunity to not just observe but actively participate in the creation of art.

Afternoon: Lunch at a Local Artisan Café
Enjoy a leisurely lunch at a local artisan café. Many cafés in Niagara Falls collaborate with local artists to showcase their works on the walls. It's a chance to relish local flavors while surrounded by creative expressions.

Evening: Artisan Market at the Outlet Collection
Explore the Outlet Collection at Niagara, which often hosts artisan markets. Browse through handmade crafts, paintings, and sculptures created by local artisans. It's an

excellent opportunity to pick up unique souvenirs and support the local art community.

Romantic Itinerary

Embarking on a romantic journey to Niagara Falls promises not only the breathtaking views of the iconic falls but also a plethora of intimate experiences that create lasting memories. This detailed itinerary is designed for couples seeking a perfect blend of romance, adventure, and relaxation during their visit to this natural wonder.

Day 1: Arrival and Evening Elegance

Morning:
Begin your romantic escape with a leisurely morning. Arrive at your chosen accommodation, preferably a cozy bed and breakfast overlooking the falls. Take a moment to savor the anticipation of the days ahead as you enjoy a delightful breakfast together.

Afternoon:
Start your afternoon with a stroll through Queen Victoria Park. Revel in the beauty of the manicured gardens and pause to absorb the panoramic views of the falls. Consider a visit to the nearby Butterfly Conservatory for a whimsical and enchanting experience surrounded by colorful butterflies.

Evening:
As the sun sets, indulge in a romantic dinner at a waterfront restaurant. The glow of the falls illuminated against the night sky sets the stage for a magical evening. Afterward, take a moonlit walk along the falls, enjoying the nightly illumination that transforms the cascading waters into a mesmerizing display of colors.

Day 2: Adventure and Bonding

Morning:
Kick off the day with an adrenaline-pumping adventure. Opt for a thrilling helicopter ride over the falls for a unique perspective that will leave you both in awe. Capture the moments with a tandem photo session, creating memories that you can cherish forever.

Afternoon:
Continue the adventure with a jet boat tour, navigating the rapids of the Niagara River. The exhilarating experience will not only add an adrenaline rush but also give you a shared sense of accomplishment. Afterward, enjoy a casual lunch at one of the local eateries, sharing stories of your adventurous escapades.

Evening:
For a more intimate and private experience, consider a sunset cruise. Drift along the river, taking in the hues of the setting sun reflecting on the falls. Choose a cruise that offers a candlelit dinner, creating a romantic ambiance as you sail beneath the stars.

Day 3: Serenity and Connection

Morning:
Indulge in a peaceful morning by exploring Niagara Glen Nature Reserve. Take a nature walk hand in hand, exploring the trails that lead to scenic overlooks of the river and gorge. Pack a picnic to enjoy in a secluded spot, surrounded by the tranquility of nature.

Afternoon:
For an afternoon of culture and art, visit local galleries or attend a live performance. Niagara-on-the-Lake, a short drive away, offers charming art studios and theaters. Explore

the quaint streets, stopping at a cafe for a leisurely afternoon coffee or tea.

Evening:
Dine at a romantic, candlelit restaurant in Niagara-on-the-Lake. The town's charming atmosphere, combined with delectable cuisine, sets the perfect tone for a romantic evening. Consider attending a live music performance or a play for an added touch of entertainment.

Day 4: Exploration and Culinary Delights

Morning:
Embark on a day of exploration by visiting the historic Fort Niagara State Park on the American side. Wander through the fort's grounds and enjoy the scenic views of Lake Ontario. Engage in activities such as bird watching or simply revel in the historical charm.

Afternoon:
For lunch, savor local flavors at one of the hidden gem restaurants. Discover the culinary delights of the region, from fresh seafood to farm-to-table dishes. Allow your taste buds to be delighted by the diverse and delicious offerings.

Evening:
Return to Niagara Falls for a romantic evening at a waterfront restaurant. Watch the falls shimmering in the background as you enjoy a gourmet dinner. Afterward, take a moonlit walk along the falls, allowing the natural beauty to enhance the romantic ambiance.

Day 5: Relaxation and Reflection

Morning:

For a serene start to your day, indulge in a couples' spa experience. Choose a spa that offers a view of the falls, allowing you both to unwind while surrounded by the soothing sounds of nature. Enjoy a massage or a wellness treatment designed to enhance relaxation.

Afternoon:
After the spa, take a leisurely drive along the Niagara Parkway. Stop at scenic viewpoints and capture moments with photos. Enjoy a casual lunch at a charming roadside cafe, savoring the simplicity of the moment.

Evening:
As your romantic getaway draws to a close, savor a farewell dinner at a romantic restaurant with a view. Reflect on the experiences shared during your time at Niagara Falls, recalling the adventures, the quiet moments, and the laughter that defined your journey.

Conclusion:

This romantic itinerary for Niagara Falls is crafted to provide a perfect balance of adventure, serenity, and connection. From the thrill of helicopter rides and jet boat tours to the quietude of nature reserves and intimate dinners, each day is designed to enhance the bond between you and your partner. Niagara Falls, with its natural beauty and romantic ambiance, serves as the ideal backdrop for a memorable and enchanting getaway for two.

Food and Wine Itinerary

This detailed itinerary spans several days, ensuring you savor the culinary delights and exquisite wines that complement the natural beauty of the falls.

Day 1: Culinary Introduction

Morning:

Start your culinary adventure with a hearty breakfast at a local cafe. Dive into fluffy pancakes drizzled with locally sourced maple syrup or opt for a classic eggs Benedict paired with freshly brewed Niagara coffee.

Late Morning:

Embark on a guided food tour through the charming town, exploring local markets and boutique stores. Sample artisanal cheeses, freshly baked pastries, and handcrafted chocolates. Engage with local producers, learning about the region's rich agricultural heritage.

Afternoon:

For lunch, choose a farm-to-table restaurant. Revel in dishes crafted from seasonal, locally grown ingredients. Pair your meal with a crisp Niagara white wine, setting the stage for a delightful culinary journey.

Evening:

Enjoy dinner at a fine dining establishment with a view of the falls. Savor a meticulously prepared tasting menu, featuring both Canadian and international influences. Pair each course with carefully selected Niagara wines, immersing yourself in a gastronomic experience as the falls are illuminated in the background.

Day 2: Wine Country Excursion

Morning:

Venture into the Niagara wine region, where lush vineyards stretch as far as the eye can see. Begin your day with a vineyard tour and wine tasting at a renowned winery. Learn about the winemaking process while sipping on exquisite vintages.

Late Morning:

Indulge in a leisurely brunch at a winery's restaurant. Delight in dishes that incorporate local ingredients, perfectly complemented by the winery's signature blends. Enjoy panoramic views of the vineyards, creating a picturesque backdrop for your meal.

Afternoon:

Explore more wineries along the Niagara Wine Route. Engage in additional tastings, discovering the nuances of different grape varietals. Consider participating in a wine blending workshop, where you can create your own custom bottle.

Evening:

Cap off your day with a wine-paired dinner at a vineyard estate. Allow the flavors of each course to dance on your palate as you overlook the sun setting over the vineyards. Immerse yourself in the romance of the wine country ambiance.

Day 3: Culinary Adventures

Morning:

Begin your day with a visit to a local farmers' market. Engage with vendors offering fresh produce, artisanal cheeses, and handmade crafts. Pick up ingredients for a picnic later in the day.

Late Morning:

Participate in a cooking class led by a local chef. Learn to prepare dishes inspired by Niagara's culinary heritage. Enjoy the fruits of your labor as you savor your creations for lunch.

Afternoon:

Take a scenic drive along the Niagara Parkway, stopping at designated picnic spots. Unwind with a gourmet picnic, relishing the flavors of local cheeses, charcuterie, and freshly baked bread. Pair your picnic with a chilled Niagara ice wine.

Evening:

For dinner, explore the diverse dining scene in the town. Choose a restaurant that piques your culinary curiosity, whether it's a cozy bistro or an ethnic eatery. Conclude your meal with a dessert showcasing the region's famous fruit, the Niagara peach.

Day 4: Fusion of Flavors

Morning:

Embark on a cultural and culinary tour, visiting neighborhoods that showcase the region's diversity. Sample international cuisines, from Italian to Indian, and learn about the culinary influences that have shaped the local food scene.

Late Morning:

Engage in a wine and cheese pairing workshop. Discover the art of harmonizing flavors, enhancing your palate with the perfect combination of wine and cheese.

Afternoon:

Spend the afternoon exploring Niagara-on-the-Lake, a charming town known for its historic architecture and boutique shops. Stop for a light lunch at a sidewalk cafe, enjoying the town's laid-back atmosphere.

Evening:

Conclude your culinary journey with a farewell dinner at a restaurant that offers a fusion of global flavors. Delight in dishes that seamlessly blend culinary traditions, creating a symphony of tastes. Toast to the conclusion of your gastronomic adventure with a glass of sparkling Niagara wine.

This four-day food and wine itinerary for Niagara Falls ensures a delightful blend of gourmet experiences, wine tastings, and cultural exploration. As you savor the local flavors and bask in the natural wonder of the falls, you'll leave with not only a visual memory of the cascading waters but a taste of the region's vibrant culinary landscape. Enjoy every bite and sip on this immersive journey through Niagara Falls' culinary delights.

Historical Itinerary

When planning a visit to the mesmerizing Niagara Falls, it's easy to get caught up in the beauty of the natural wonder itself. However, the region is also steeped in a rich history that spans centuries. Embark on a historical journey through time with this detailed itinerary, carefully crafted to offer a blend of educational insights and captivating experiences.

Day 1: Indigenous Heritage and Early Explorers

Morning:

1. Start at the Niagara Falls History Museum: Begin your historical exploration at the Niagara Falls History Museum. Delve into exhibits that trace the region's Indigenous roots, the arrival of European explorers, and the development of the falls as a tourist attraction.

2. Indigenous Cultural Center: Immerse yourself in the vibrant culture and history of the Indigenous peoples of the area. Learn about their traditions, art, and the profound connection they have with the land.

Afternoon:

3. Lunch at Queenston Heights: Head to Queenston Heights Park for a scenic lunch. This site has historical significance as the location of the Battle of Queenston Heights during the War of 1812.

4. Brock's Monument: After lunch, visit Brock's Monument, a towering tribute to Major General Sir Isaac Brock, a key figure in the War of 1812. Climb to the top for panoramic views of the Niagara region.

Evening:

5. Dinner at The Old Winery Restaurant: Conclude the day with dinner at The Old Winery Restaurant, housed in a building dating back to 1888. Enjoy local cuisine in a historic setting.

Day 2: War of 1812 and the Underground Railroad

Morning:

1. Fort George National Historic Site: Explore Fort George, a military post from the War of 1812. Engage in interactive exhibits and witness reenactments that bring the past to life.
2. Laura Secord Homestead: Visit the home of Laura Secord, a Canadian heroine from the War of 1812. Learn about her courageous journey to warn British forces of an American attack.

Afternoon:

3. Lunch at The Angel Inn: Dine at The Angel Inn, a historic pub in Niagara-on-the-Lake dating back to the early 19th century. The inn has welcomed notable figures, including Winston Churchill.

4. Visit the Niagara Historical Society Museum: Discover more about the region's history at the Niagara Historical Society Museum. Exhibits cover the War of 1812, early settlers, and the development of Niagara-on-the-Lake.

Evening:

5. Jet Boating Night Tour: Experience the thrill of a night jet boat tour. While exhilarating, it also highlights the historic significance of the Niagara River, including its role in the Underground Railroad.

Day 3: Industrialization and Innovation
Morning:

1. Breakfast at The Flour Mill Restaurant: Begin your day at The Flour Mill Restaurant, located in an old flour mill that dates back to 1904. Enjoy a hearty breakfast in a historic industrial setting.

2. Lock 3 and Welland Canals Centre: Explore the Welland Canal, a marvel of engineering that played a pivotal role in industrial transportation. The Lock 3 viewing platform offers a close-up look at the canal's operation.
Afternoon:

3. Lunch at The Syndicate Restaurant: Dine at The Syndicate Restaurant, housed in a building that once served as the Dominion Bank. Admire the historic architecture while savoring a meal.

4. Niagara Parks Power Station: Take a guided tour of the Niagara Parks Power Station, a hydroelectric facility dating back to 1905. Learn about the role of hydroelectric power in the region's industrial development.

Evening:

5. Dinner at Windows by Jamie Kennedy: Enjoy dinner at Windows by Jamie Kennedy, located in the Sheraton Fallsview Hotel. This modern restaurant offers panoramic views and celebrates the region's agricultural and culinary heritage.

Day 4: Modern Marvels and Preservation Efforts

'Morning:

1. Breakfast at The Old Powerhouse Restaurant: Start your day with breakfast at The Old Powerhouse Restaurant, located in a historic building that once housed a power station.

2. Niagara Glen Nature Centre: Explore the Niagara Glen, a protected nature reserve. The Niagara Glen Nature Centre

provides insights into the preservation efforts and ecological significance of the area.

Afternoon:

3. Lunch at Elements on the Falls: Dine at Elements on the Falls, located in Table Rock Centre. Enjoy a meal with stunning views of the falls and learn about the conservation efforts to protect this natural wonder.

4. Journey Behind the Falls: Experience the Journey Behind the Falls, an attraction with historical tunnels that take you behind the cascading waters. Gain insights into the early infrastructure developed to access and appreciate the falls.

Evening:

5. Dinner at Revolving Dining Room: Conclude your historical journey with dinner at the Revolving Dining Room in the Skylon Tower. Marvel at the panoramic views of the falls and reflect on the historical evolution of this iconic destination.

This detailed historical itinerary offers a diverse exploration of the Niagara Falls region, from its Indigenous roots and early explorers to its pivotal role in the War of 1812, industrialization, and modern conservation efforts. Each day is designed to provide a balanced mix of educational experiences and memorable moments in this captivating historical landscape.

Outdoor Adventure Itinerary

When planning an outdoor adventure around the Niagara Falls, the possibilities are as vast as the falls themselves. From thrilling water experiences to scenic hikes and cultural discoveries, this itinerary is designed to make the most of your visit. Get ready for an action-packed journey spanning several days, each filled with unique activities that showcase the beauty and excitement of the Niagara Falls region.

Day 1: Thrills on the Water

Morning:

Maid of the Mist Experience: Start your adventure with an iconic boat tour that takes you up close to the thundering waters of Niagara Falls. Feel the mist on your face as you navigate the powerful currents, gaining a perspective that few get to experience.

Afternoon:

Jet Boating Adventure: For an adrenaline rush, embark on a jet boating adventure on the Niagara River. Brace yourself for thrilling spins and heart-pounding maneuvers as you navigate through the Class V rapids. It's a wet and wild experience that adds an extra layer of excitement to your day.

Evening:

Dinner with a View: Wind down your day with a relaxing dinner at a waterfront restaurant. Choose a spot with panoramic views of the falls to enjoy a delicious meal while basking in the illuminated beauty of the falls at night.

Day 2: Land and Sky Adventures

Morning:

Morning Hike to Niagara Glen: Lace up your hiking boots and head to Niagara Glen Nature Reserve. Explore the scenic trails that lead to stunning viewpoints overlooking the Niagara River. Challenge yourself with the Whirlpool Rapids Trail for a more adventurous hike.

Afternoon:

Ziplining Across the Gorge: Experience the thrill of ziplining over the Niagara Gorge. Soar through the air and take in breathtaking views of the river below. It's an exhilarating way to add an adrenaline-pumping activity to your day.

Evening:

Sunset Biking Adventure: Rent bikes and explore the Niagara Parkway. As the sun sets, pedal along the riverside, enjoying the changing colors of the sky and the tranquil beauty of the surroundings.

Day 3: Exploring Beyond the Falls

Morning:

Day Trip to Niagara-on-the-Lake: Venture beyond the falls and spend a day exploring the charming town of Niagara-on-the-Lake. Known for its historic architecture, boutique shops, and wineries, it offers a delightful change of pace.

Afternoon:

Winery Tour: Niagara-on-the-Lake is renowned for its wineries. Join a wine tour to sample the region's best vintages while enjoying picturesque vineyard views.

Evening:

Dinner in the Old Town: Wrap up your day with a romantic dinner in the Old Town. Choose a cozy restaurant with a patio to savor your meal in a charming outdoor setting.

Day 4: Family-Friendly Fun

Morning:

Adventure Park Excursion: If you're traveling with family, spend the morning at an adventure park near the falls. Enjoy zip-lining, rope courses, and other family-friendly activities.

Afternoon:

Butterfly Conservatory: Immerse yourself in the beauty of the Butterfly Conservatory. Wander through lush gardens while colorful butterflies flutter around you, creating a magical and educational experience for both kids and adults.

Evening:

Family-Friendly Dining: Choose a family-friendly restaurant on Clifton Hill, known for its vibrant atmosphere and diverse dining options.

Day 5: Nature and Relaxation

Morning:

Visit Dufferin Islands: Start your day with a visit to Dufferin Islands, a tranquil retreat just south of the falls. Stroll through scenic paths, cross charming bridges, and enjoy the peaceful ambiance of this hidden gem.

Afternoon:

Picnic by the River: Pack a picnic and find a serene spot along the Niagara River. Enjoy a leisurely lunch surrounded by nature, taking in the beauty of the river and the distant falls.

Evening:

Sunset Yoga: Unwind with a sunset yoga session overlooking the falls. Many parks in the area offer open spaces for yoga, providing a perfect way to connect with nature and relax your mind.

Day 6: Cultural and Historical Exploration

Morning:

Explore Old Fort Niagara: Delve into history with a visit to Old Fort Niagara on the American side. Explore the well-preserved buildings, artifacts, and scenic views of Lake Ontario.

Afternoon:

Lunch in Lewiston: Head to the nearby town of Lewiston for lunch. This charming village offers a mix of historic charm and modern cuisine, making it a delightful stop on your cultural exploration.

Evening:

Artpark and Outdoor Concert: If your visit coincides with an event at Artpark, an outdoor amphitheater, catch a live performance under the stars. It's a unique cultural experience surrounded by nature.

Day 7: Relaxation and Reflection

Morning:

Spa Day: Treat yourself to a spa day at one of the luxurious spas in the area. Rejuvenate with massages, facials, and other wellness treatments.

Afternoon:

Quiet Time at Oakes Garden Theatre: Spend a peaceful afternoon at Oakes Garden Theatre. This beautifully landscaped garden offers a serene environment for reflection and relaxation.

Evening:

Farewell Dinner Cruise: Conclude your adventure with a farewell dinner cruise. Sail along the Niagara River, enjoying a gourmet meal with the falls as your backdrop. It's a magical way to end your outdoor exploration of the Niagara Falls region.

This comprehensive itinerary ensures that every day of your visit is filled with exciting outdoor activities, stunning natural scenery, and cultural discoveries. Whether you're seeking adventure, relaxation, or a bit of both, the Niagara Falls region offers a diverse range of experiences for outdoor enthusiasts.

Chapter 21: Planning Your Next Visit

Tips for Return Travelers

Familiarity with the area certainly has its perks, but there's always more to discover and new experiences to savor. Here are some valuable tips to make your return trip even more memorable:

1. Explore Different Seasons:

One of the wonders of Niagara Falls is its ever-changing beauty throughout the seasons. If your previous visit was in the summer, consider coming back during the fall to witness the vibrant foliage, or brave the winter chill for a magical frozen falls experience. Each season brings its own unique charm.

2. Take Advantage of Loyalty Programs:

Many local businesses and attractions offer loyalty programs for returning visitors. Check for discounts, special packages, or exclusive perks that come with being a repeat guest. It's a great way to save on your favorite activities.

3. Engage with the Local Community:

Returning to Niagara Falls gives you the opportunity to go beyond the tourist hotspots and engage with the local community. Attend community events, visit local markets, and strike up conversations with residents. You'll uncover hidden gems and gain a deeper appreciation for the area's culture.

4. Try New Adventures:

Even if you've checked off many items from your bucket list on your first visit, there's always something new to try. Seek out activities or attractions you missed the first time, or be adventurous and try something completely different. The Falls are a treasure trove of exciting experiences.

5. Stay Updated on Events:

Niagara Falls hosts a variety of events throughout the year, from music festivals to cultural celebrations. Stay updated on the event calendar and plan your visit around something that piques your interest. It's a fantastic way to infuse your trip with a dose of local flavor.

6. Connect with Fellow Travelers:

Join travel forums or social media groups dedicated to Niagara Falls enthusiasts. Share your experiences, seek recommendations, and connect with fellow travelers. Their insights might lead you to hidden spots and insider tips you wouldn't discover on your own.

7. Extend Your Stay:

If possible, consider extending your stay beyond your previous visit. This allows for a more relaxed exploration, giving you the freedom to delve deeper into the attractions you love and discover new favorites along the way.

8. Support Sustainable Tourism:

As a returning traveler, consider ways to contribute to the sustainability of this beautiful destination. Choose eco-friendly activities, support local businesses that prioritize sustainability, and leave a positive impact on the environment.

9. Capture New Memories:

Bring your camera or smartphone and capture fresh moments. Whether it's the changing colors of the landscape, candid shots of locals, or a new perspective of the Falls, creating a new set of memories will make your return trip distinct from the previous one.

10. Reflect and Reconnect:

Take some time during your return trip to reflect on your previous experiences. Revisit places that held special meaning for you and take a moment to appreciate the personal growth and joy that travel brings. It's a chance to reconnect with the essence of your initial journey.

Returning to Niagara Falls is like revisiting an old friend—with each encounter, the bond deepens, and the connection becomes richer. Use these tips to make your return trip a delightful blend of nostalgia and discovery. Happy travels!

Seasonal Highlights

As the seasons change around Niagara Falls, so does the landscape, atmosphere, and the array of activities available. Each season brings a unique charm to the region, ensuring there's always something exciting for visitors to experience. Let's delve into the seasonal highlights that make each visit to Niagara Falls a fresh and enchanting adventure.

Spring: Blooms and Renewal

Spring in Niagara is a symphony of colors and fragrances. The falls come to life as the surrounding gardens burst into bloom. Tulips, daffodils, and cherry blossoms paint a vibrant picture against the backdrop of the rushing waters. Spring is an ideal time for hiking and exploring the natural beauty surrounding the falls. The weather is mild, and the air is filled with the invigorating scent of new beginnings.

Summer: Festival Season

As the days get longer and warmer, Niagara transforms into a festival haven. The Summer Festival of Lights illuminates the falls and surrounding areas with captivating light displays. Music festivals, food events, and outdoor concerts offer entertainment for all tastes. Adventure seekers can enjoy water activities to cool off, while families can explore the many parks and family-friendly attractions.

Fall: A Tapestry of Colors

Autumn blankets Niagara in a rich tapestry of reds, yellows, and oranges. The falls provide a stunning backdrop to the changing foliage. Fall is harvest season, bringing with it a plethora of fresh produce and culinary delights. Visitors can embark on scenic drives through wine country, savoring the flavors of local vineyards. The crisp air and fewer crowds make fall an excellent time for romantic getaways.

Winter: Frozen Wonderlands

Niagara's winter transforms the region into a magical wonderland. The falls may partially freeze, creating a breathtaking icy spectacle. Winter sports enthusiasts can enjoy ice skating near the falls or venture to nearby slopes for skiing and snowboarding. Cozy up in front of fireplaces in local inns, sip hot cocoa, and take in the serene beauty of a winter wonderland.

Seasonal Transitions: Capturing the In-Between

The transitions between seasons in Niagara are equally captivating. Spring transitioning to summer brings the roar of waterfalls complemented by the melodies of songbirds. Fall into winter brings the anticipation of holiday festivities and the first snowfall. These in-between periods offer a unique blend of experiences, allowing visitors to witness the transformation of the landscape.

Tips for Seasonal Exploration:

- Check Event Calendars: Many seasonal events and festivals are held throughout the year. Check local event calendars to align your visit with exciting activities.

- Dress Accordingly: Niagara experiences all four seasons distinctly. Pack accordingly to make the most of your visit, whether it's sunscreen and light clothing in summer or layers and warm jackets in winter.

- Book Accommodations in Advance: Some seasons, especially summer and fall, attract more visitors. Booking accommodations in advance ensures you secure the best options and enjoy a stress-free stay.

- Embrace Seasonal Cuisine: Local restaurants often feature seasonal menus. Embrace the flavors of the season by trying dishes made from fresh, local ingredients.

Making Lasting Memories

As your time near the captivating Niagara Falls draws to a close, it's essential to reflect on the moments that will linger in your memory for a lifetime. The Niagara experience is more than just a series of attractions; it's an opportunity to create lasting memories that will stay with you long after you've left the misty embrace of the falls.

Capturing the Perfect Moments

Niagara Falls offers a myriad of picturesque settings for capturing the perfect photographs. Take a stroll along the Niagara Parkway at different times of the day to witness the falls transform under various lights. The early morning sun casting a golden glow on the water or the falls illuminated by colorful lights at night — each moment presents a unique photo opportunity.

Don't forget to capture candid shots of your companions against the backdrop of the falls. These genuine moments of joy and amazement will be the ones you cherish the most when reminiscing about your visit.

Keepsakes and Souvenirs

Bring a piece of Niagara home with you through carefully chosen keepsakes and souvenirs. Whether it's a handcrafted trinket from a local artisan, a personalized item from the falls' gift shops, or a photo book documenting your journey, these tangible reminders will transport you back to the excitement and wonder of your time at Niagara Falls.

Consider picking up a unique piece of artwork or a locally crafted item that reflects the spirit of the region. Not only do these items make excellent conversation starters, but they also serve as tangible connections to the memories you've created.

Journaling Your Adventures

Take a moment each day to jot down your thoughts and experiences in a travel journal. Documenting your adventures, the people you meet, and the emotions you feel adds a personal touch to your journey. Years from now, reading through your entries will transport you back to the excitement and wonder of exploring Niagara Falls.

Include details about the unexpected discoveries, the flavors of the local cuisine, and the sounds of the falls in your journal. It's a simple yet effective way to preserve the nuances of your trip that may fade from memory over time.

Reflecting on Moments of Serenity

Amidst the excitement and thrill of the various activities around Niagara Falls, take a moment to find a quiet spot and simply absorb the natural beauty around you. Whether it's a secluded spot in a park or a peaceful gazebo overlooking the river, these moments of serenity will become treasured memories.

Close your eyes, listen to the rhythmic sound of the falls, and breathe in the fresh mist-filled air. These peaceful interludes will serve as mental snapshots, allowing you to revisit the tranquility of Niagara whenever life gets hectic.

Connecting with Locals

One of the most enriching aspects of travel is the opportunity to connect with the locals. Strike up conversations with shop owners, tour guides, and fellow travelers. Learn about the history and traditions of the area from those who call it home. These personal connections often result in heartwarming stories and shared laughter, leaving you with a deeper appreciation for the destination.

As you bid farewell to Niagara Falls, take a moment to appreciate the memories you've created. Whether it's the exhilaration of a boat ride to the base of the falls, the taste of local delicacies, or the simple joy of sharing the experience with loved ones, Niagara Falls has woven itself into the fabric of your life's adventures, leaving you with a tapestry of lasting memories.

Made in the USA
Middletown, DE
08 August 2024